D0140197

2021-2022 Supplement

National Security Law
Seventh Edition

and

Counterterrorism Law
Fourth Edition

EDITORIAL ADVISORS

Rachel E. Barkow
Segal Family Professor of Regulatory Law and Policy
Faculty Director, Center on the Administration of Criminal Law
New York University School of Law

Erwin Chemerinsky
Dean and Jesse H. Choper Distinguished Professor of Law
University of California, Berkeley School of Law

Richard A. Epstein
Laurence A. Tisch Professor of Law
New York University School of Law
Peter and Kirsten Bedford Senior Fellow
The Hoover Institution
Senior Lecturer in Law
The University of Chicago

Ronald J. Gilson
Charles J. Meyers Professor of Law and Business
Stanford University
Marc and Eva Stern Professor of Law and Business
Columbia Law School

James E. Krier
Earl Warren DeLano Professor of Law
The University of Michigan Law School

Tracey L. Meares
Walton Hale Hamilton Professor of Law
Director, The Justice Collaboratory
Yale Law School

Richard K. Neumann, Jr.
Alexander Bickel Professor of Law
Maurice A. Deane School of Law at Hofstra University

Robert H. Sitkoff
John L. Gray Professor of Law
Harvard Law School

David Alan Sklansky
Stanley Morrison Professor of Law
Faculty Co-Director, Stanford Criminal Justice Center
Stanford Law School

2021–2022 Supplement

National Security Law
Seventh Edition

and

Counterterrorism Law
Fourth Edition

Stephen Dycus
Professor Emeritus
Vermont Law School

William C. Banks
College of Law Board of Advisors Distinguished Professor
Syracuse University College of Law

Emily Berman
Associate Professor
University of Houston Law Center

Peter Raven-Hansen
Glen Earl Weston Research Professor of Law Emeritus
George Washington University

Stephen I. Vladeck
Charles Alan Wright Chair in Federal Courts
University of Texas School of Law

Copyright © 2021 Stephen Dycus, William C. Banks, Emily Berman, Peter Raven-Hansen, and Stephen I. Vladeck.

Published by Wolters Kluwer in New York.

Wolters Kluwer Legal & Regulatory U.S. serves customers worldwide with CCH, Aspen Publishers, and Kluwer Law International products. (www.WKLegaledu.com)

No part of this publication may be reproduced or transmitted in any form or by any means, electronic or mechanical, including photocopy, recording, or utilized by any information storage or retrieval system, without written permission from the publisher. For information about permissions or to request permissions online, visit us at www.WKLegaledu.com, or a written request may be faxed to our permissions department at 212-771-0803.

To contact Customer Service, e-mail customer.service@wolterskluwer.com, call 1-800-234-1660, fax 1-800-901-9075, or mail correspondence to:

Wolters Kluwer
Attn: Order Department
PO Box 990
Frederick, MD 21705

Printed in the United States of America.

1 2 3 4 5 6 7 8 9 0

ISBN 978-1-5438-2034-8

About Wolters Kluwer Legal & Regulatory U.S.

Wolters Kluwer Legal & Regulatory U.S. delivers expert content and solutions in the areas of law, corporate compliance, health compliance, reimbursement, and legal education. Its practical solutions help customers successfully navigate the demands of a changing environment to drive their daily activities, enhance decision quality and inspire confident outcomes.

Serving customers worldwide, its legal and regulatory portfolio includes products under the Aspen Publishers, CCH Incorporated, Kluwer Law International, ftwilliam.com and MediRegs names. They are regarded as exceptional and trusted resources for general legal and practice-specific knowledge, compliance and risk management, dynamic workflow solutions, and expert commentary.

***

Contents

Contents

Contents

***

Preface

For most casebooks, the immediate aftermath of a new edition is relatively calm, with little need to quickly address new developments, and even less likelihood of multiple field-shifting events following shortly on the heels of publication. But as is so often true in the fields of National Security Law and Counterterrorism Law, and has so often been true for the *National Security Law* and *Counterterrorism Law* casebooks for which this *Supplement* exists, the last year has been . . . busy. Indeed, the new content in this *Supplement* runs to a total of 142 pages. Not only has the COVID-19 pandemic raised many important, novel, and complex legal questions about governmental emergency powers, especially in the field of public health, but the 2020 election and its violent aftermath have likewise surfaced (or resurfaced) long-running debates over the difference between international and domestic terrorism — and how (if at all) the authorities for the former can and should be mapped onto the latter.

Nor are these questions entirely in the rear-view mirror. As this *Supplement* goes to press, for example, litigation is ongoing over many of the state and federal responses to COVID-19, and the criminal cases arising out of the January 6 violence at the U.S. Capitol continue to produce new and interesting judicial decisions that, in some cases, must construe long-dormant statutory authorities. Meanwhile, the Supreme Court is set to consider during its October 2021 term its first-ever case about the Foreign Intelligence Surveillance Act (FISA), along with a major case about the state secrets privilege as it relates to the CIA's torture of terrorism suspects overseas in the first years after the September 11 attacks.

Speaking of FISA, there have also been a number of important new developments on that front in all three branches of government — including curious decisions by Congress to allow surveillance authorities that had expanded dramatically after September 11 to either revert to their pre-9/11 form or completely expire. The *Supplement* addresses these developments in detail, as well.

And, of course, there is still the ongoing military detention and military commission regimes at Guantánamo, where 40 men remain in custody as this *Supplement* goes to press. New in this *Supplement* is detailed coverage of the *Al-Hela* case — in which the en banc D.C. Circuit is set to hear argument in September 2021, and which may have major implications not just for Guantánamo habeas cases, but for the constitutional rights of non-citizens outside the United States more generally.

As ever, we have tried to keep up with these and many other developments without overly complicating the use of the core casebooks. Achieving that practical goal necessarily requires discriminating selection and presentation. As in past supplements, we have carefully edited the principal new cases and supplied a minimum of new Notes and Questions, trusting our enterprising adopters to use (and embellish) them as they feel best fits their teaching goals.

To aid us in this project, we have also brought onboard a terrific new co-author, Professor Emily Berman from the University of Houston Law Center, who adds her formidable professional and academic background and cutting-edge scholarship to our cohort.

This *Supplement* serves two closely related casebooks: *National Security Law* (7th ed. 2020) and *Counterterrorism Law* (4th ed. 2020). This Preface is followed immediately by two Teacher's Guides, one for each book, which indicate the placement of supplemental materials within each casebook (and are intended to make it easier for adopters to match *Supplement* entries to their syllabi). Each document in the *Supplement* is accompanied by a reference to one or both casebooks, depending on where the relevant underlying material appears. For example, the insert concerning the ongoing dispute over the government's reliance upon evidence obtained through torture in one of the Guantánamo military commission prosecutions appears with this instruction: **[NSL p. 1156, CTL p. 808. Insert after Note 6.]** "NSL" refers to *National Security Law* (7th ed.), and "CTL" to *Counterterrorism Law* (4th ed.).

As important new developments arise during the coming year, we will continue to document them by posting edited new materials on the websites for the two casebooks — supplements to this *Supplement* — from which they may be downloaded by teachers and shared with students. The website for *National Security Law* (7th ed.) may be found at https://www.wklegaledu.com/Dycus-NationalSec7; the website for *Counterterrorism Law* (4th ed.) may be found at https://www.wklegaledu.com/Dycus-Counterterrorism4. For each book, log in with a validated professor account for access to our materials.

However, adopters are forewarned that when events move as quickly as they have in our field, the first responsibility for keeping up lies with them. Thus, the adopter who wishes to discuss the implications of the January 6, 2021 riots for domestic terrorism laws, or the government's authority to buy third-party data or to obtain the metadata of journalists in a leak investigation, should consider the materials in the casebooks and this *Supplement* as, at most, a platform for discussion, on which they must build with contemporaneous materials that they themselves locate and curate from the media and from the wonderful national security blogs available to them. (And, when they do, share them with us!)

As always, we are extremely grateful to our adopters, fellow members of the National Security Law Section of the Association of American Law Schools, fellow members of the Editorial Board of the *Journal of National Security Law & Policy*, fellow casebook authors (our collaborators in building the field), members of the ABA Standing Committee on Law and National Security, and our many friends in the national security community. We also wish to thank our research assistants. Finally, we wish to express our gratitude to Carol McGeehan, John Devins, and Jeff Slutzky, our long-time editors and friends, for their encouragement and support in this work.

Stephen Dycus
William C. Banks
Emily Berman
Peter Raven-Hansen
Stephen I. Vladeck

July 15, 2021

Teacher's Guide for National Security Law (7th edition)

Chapter 9. *International Humanitarian Law (jus in bello)*

Chapter 11. *Collective Use of Force*

Chapter 12. *Unilateral Use of Force*

Chapter 13. *Targeting Terrorists*

Chapter 14. *Cyber Operations*

Chapter 15. *Nuclear War*

Chapter 24. The Collection and Use of Third-Party Records

Chapter 25. Screening for Security

Chapter 26. Profiling and Travel Bans

Chapter 28. Habeas Corpus: The Scope of the Suspension Clause

Chapter 30. Military Detention of Non-U.S. Persons

Chapter 31. Preventive Detention

Chapter 33. Case Study of Coercive Interrogation of Detainees in U.S. Custody After 9/11

Chapter 34. Criminalizing Terrorism and Its Precursors

Chapter 36. Trial by Military Commission

Chapter 37. Homeland Security

Chapter 38. The Military's Domestic Role

Chapter 39. Safeguarding National Security Information

Chapter 40. Access to National Security Information

Chapter 41. Censorship

Teacher's Guide for Counterterrorism Law (4th edition)

Chapter 8. The Fourth Amendment and National Security

Chapter 9. Congressional Authority for Foreign Intelligence Surveillance

Chapter 10. Programmatic Electronic Surveillance for Foreign Intelligence

Chapter 11. The Third-Party Doctrine: Origins and Applications

Chapter 12. The Collection and Use of Third-Party Records

Chapter 13. Screening for Security

Chapter 14. Profiling and Travel Bans

Chapter 16. Habeas Corpus: The Scope of the Suspension Clause

Chapter 18. Military Detention of Non-U.S. Persons

Chapter 19. Preventive Detention

Chapter 20. Case Study of Coercive Interrogation of Detainees in U.S. Custody After 9/11

Chapter 21. Criminalizing Terrorism and Its Precursors

Chapter 24. Trial by Military Commission

Chapter 25. Homeland Security

Chapter 26. The Military's Domestic Role

Chapter 28. Suing Terrorists and Their Supporters

***

Table of Cases

***

[NSL p. 75. Insert at the end of Note 6.]

President Biden terminated the border emergency on his first day of office. Proclamation No. 10,142, *Termination of Emergency with Respect to the Southern Border of the United States and Redirection of Funds Diverted to Border Wall Construction*, 86 Fed. Reg. 7225 (Jan. 20, 2021). He explained that "the declaration of a national emergency at our southern border in Proclamation 9844 of February 15, 2019 (Declaring a National Emergency Concerning the Southern Border of the United States), was unwarranted." *Id.* at 7225. Does that make unlawful any acts undertaken by the prior administration under authority of that emergency? Or is it a political question whether a declaration of emergency was warranted? See Chapter 5(B)(2).

[NSL p. 107. Insert before first full paragraph. For excerpt concerning standing from the same opinion, see *infra* insert for NSL p. 140.]

U.S. House of Representatives v. Mnuchin
United States Court of Appeals, D.C. Circuit, Sept. 25, 2020
976 F.3d 1, *petition for cert. filed*, No. 20-1738 (U.S. June 15, 2021)

Before: MILLETT and WILKINS, Circuit Judges, and SENTELLE, Senior Circuit Judge.

SENTELLE, Senior Circuit Judge: The United States House of Representatives brought this lawsuit alleging that the Departments of Defense, Homeland Security, the Treasury, and the Interior, and the Secretaries of those departments violated the Appropriations Clause of the Constitution as well as the Administrative Procedure Act when transferring funds appropriated for other uses to finance the construction of a physical barrier along the southern border of the United States, contravening congressionally approved appropriations. The District Court for the District of Columbia held that it had no jurisdiction because the House lacked standing to challenge the defendants' actions as it did not allege a legally cognizable injury. We disagree as to the constitutional claims and therefore vacate and remand for further proceedings. . . .

II.

A. . . .

Underlying the present litigation is a dispute about the nature of Congress's authority under the Appropriations Clause of the Constitution and whether the President's refusal to follow the limits on his authority injures one House of Congress. The Constitution provides, "No Money shall be drawn from the Treasury, but in Consequence of Appropriations made by Law." U.S. Const. art. I, §9, cl. 7. Because the clause is phrased as a limitation, it means that "the expenditure on public funds is proper only when authorized by Congress, not that public funds may be expended unless prohibited by Congress." *United States v. MacCollom*, 426 U.S. 317, 321 (1976) (plurality opinion) (citing *Reeside v. Walker*, 52 U.S. (11 How.) 272, 291 (1851)). The Appropriations Clause, thus, provides one foundational element of the separation between the powers of the sword of the Executive Branch and the purse of the Legislative Branch. It is a core structural protection of the Constitution — a wall, so to speak, between the branches of government that prevents encroachment of the House's and Senate's power of the purse. *See Freytag v. Comm'r*, 501 U.S. 868, 878 (1991) ("Our separation-of-powers jurisprudence generally focuses on the danger of one branch's aggrandizing its power at the expense of another branch."); *see also Free Enter. Fund v. Pub. Co. Accounting Oversight Bd.*, 561 U.S. 477, 501 (2010) ("The Framers created a structure . . . giving each branch 'the necessary constitutional means, and personal motives, to resist encroachments of the others[.]'") (quoting *The Federalist* No. 48 at 333; and No. 51 at 349 (J. Madison)) (internal citations omitted); *cf. Plaut v. Spendthrift Farm, Inc.*, 514 U.S. 211, 239 (1995) ("[T]he doctrine of separation of powers is a *structural safeguard* . . . establishing high walls and clear distinctions.") (emphasis in original).

The separation between the Executive and the ability to appropriate funds was frequently cited during the founding era as the premier check on the President's power. In fact, "the separation of purse and sword was the Federalists' strongest rejoinder to Anti-Federalist fears of a tyrannical president." Josh Chafetz, *Congress's Constitution, Legislative Authority and the Separation of Powers* 57 (2017); *see also* 3 *The Debates in the Several State Conventions on the Adoption of the Federal Constitution* 367 (Jonathan Elliot ed., 2d ed. 1836) (hereinafter *Debates*) (responding to charges that the President could easily become king by explaining that "[t]he purse is in the hands of the representatives of the people"). For example, James Madison, in the Federalist Papers, explained, "Th[e] power over the purse may in fact be regarded as the most compleat and effectual weapon with which any constitution can arm the immediate representatives of the people . . . ." *The Federalist* No. 58 at 394 (J. Madison) (Jacob E. Cooke ed., 1961). At the New York ratification convention, Alexander Hamilton reassured listeners, stating, "where the purse is lodged in one branch, and the sword in another, there can be no danger." 2 *Debates* 349.

As evidenced by the quotations above, a repeated theme in the founding era was the importance of putting the power of the purse specifically in the hands of the "representatives of the people." *The Federalist* No. 58 at 394 (J. Madison) (Jacob E. Cooke ed., 1961); 2 *Debates* 393. As noted above, an early draft of the Constitution went as far as to require [that] appropriations bills originate in the House of Representatives, the representatives of the people. 2 *Records* 131. While the final text does not include that same origination provision and provides only that "[a]ll bills for raising Revenue shall originate in the House of Representatives," U.S. Const. art. I, §7, cl. 1, "[u]nder immemorial custom the general appropriations bills . . . originate in the House of Representatives." *Cannon's Procedure in the House of Representatives* 20, §834 (4th ed. 1944). In fact, "the House has returned to the Senate a Senate bill or joint resolution appropriating money on the ground that it invaded the prerogatives of the House." Wm. Holmes Brown, *House Practice* 71 (1996); *see also* 3 *Deschler's Precedents* 336 (1976). The appropriations statute at issue in this case originated with the House, as is traditional. 165 Cong. Rec. H997 (daily ed. Jan. 22, 2019); 165 Cong. Rec. H1181-83 (daily ed. Jan. 24, 2019). . . .

[NSL p. 121. Insert at the end of Note 1.]

Eventually, the Court of Appeals reached the merits in *Trump v. Sierra Club,* 963 F.3d 874 (9th Cir. 2020), and a companion case, *California v. Trump,* 963 F.3d 926 (9th Cir. 2020). In each case, the panel voted 2-1 to affirm partial summary judgment for the plaintiffs, and in the latter it also granted a permanent injunction. The Supreme Court then granted certiorari in *Trump v. Sierra Club.* 141 S. Ct. 618 (2020) (mem.). But after the 2020 election, the new administration terminated the border emergency and redirected funds away from the border wall construction. *See* Proclamation No. 10,142, *Termination of Emergency with Respect to the Southern Border of the United States and Redirection of Funds Diverted to Border Wall Construction,* 86 Fed. Reg. 7225 (Jan. 20, 2021). The Court then granted the government's motion to remove the case from the calendar. *Biden v. Sierra Club*, 141 S. Ct. 1289 (2021) (mem.). On July 2, after an intervening memorandum from the Secretary of Defense, the Supreme Court granted the government's motion to vacate the Ninth Circuit's judgment and remanded the case to the district court to "consider what further proceedings [are] necessary and appropriate in light of the changed circumstances in this case." *Biden v. Sierra Club*, No. 20-138, 2021 WL 2742775 (U.S. July 2, 2021) (mem.).

[NSL p. 122. Insert after Note 6.]

7. Can a New President Halt the Diversion? Incident to his termination of the border emergency that President Trump had declared (NSL p. 70), President Biden directed officials to "pause work on each construction project on the southern border wall, to the extent permitted by law ... [and to] pause immediately the obligation of funds related to construction of the southern border wall, to the extent permitted by law." Proclamation No. 10,142, *Termination of Emergency with Respect to the Southern Border of the United States and Redirection of Funds Diverted to Border Wall Construction*, 86 Fed. Reg. 7225 (Jan. 20, 2021). Did he have that authority, assuming that the funds he "paused" had been lawfully diverted from funds appropriated for other purposes? Or was the Biden hold an unlawful "impoundment" of appropriated funds, thwarting congressional intent? And if the hold was lawful, how was it different from President Trump's threatened hold on funds for Ukraine for its alleged failure to investigate Hunter Biden's activities related to that country?

The U.S. Government Accountability Office concluded that President Biden had the authority to impose the hold on border wall spending.

> We conclude that delays in the obligation and expenditure of DHS's appropriations are programmatic delays, not impoundments. DHS and the Office of Management and Budget (OMB) have shown that the use of funds is delayed in order to perform environmental reviews and consult with various stakeholders, as required by law, and determine project funding needs in light of changes that warrant using funds differently than initially planned. As explained below, because the delay here is precipitated by legal requirements, the delay is distinguishable from the withholding of Ukraine security assistance funds. [U.S. Gov't Accountability Off., *Office of Management and Budget and U.S. Department of Homeland Security —*

Pause of Border Barrier Construction and Obligations (GAO B-333110), at 1 (June 15, 2021).]

But the GAO's approval was not unequivocal. "In order to facilitate Congress's oversight of executive spending and its Constitutional power of the purse," it recommended that the relevant congressional committees submit a timeline for obligating DHS's fiscal year 2021 appropriation "to ensure the President does not substitute his own policies and priorities in place of those established through the legislative process." *Id.*

[NSL p. 138. Insert before the last paragraph in Note 2.]

The District Court in *Zaidan* eventually dismissed on grounds of the state secrets privilege (*see infra* NSL p. 154). 412 F. Supp. 3d 52 (D.D.C. 2020). On appeal of that dismissal, however, the Court of Appeals went back to standing, reasoning that it was a jurisdictional requirement that can be questioned at any point in the litigation. *Kareem v. Haspel*, 986 F.3d 859 (D.C. Cir. 2021). The court held that Kareem's complaint did not cross the line from possible to plausible, and affirmed the dismissal on this alternate ground.

Concluding that the complaint did not contain any factual allegations that explicitly linked the United States to any of the alleged airstrikes, the appeals court seemed to go out of its way to reject Kareem's inferences of attribution based on the likelihood that a Hellfire missile (of the sort launched by U.S. drones) was involved in the attacks.

> Even assuming *arguendo* that the United States was the only actor in Syria using Hellfire missiles in 2016, Kareem's allegation nonetheless suffers from two fatal flaws: (1) we cannot give the allegation material weight because Kareem has apparently retreated from the assertion in this litigation and (2) it provides no plausible inference that Kareem was the specific target of the airstrike. First, the complaint alleges that the third airstrike involved "a drone-launched Hellfire missile." But Kareem's appellate briefing undermines that factual assertion. Kareem's opening brief categorizes this airstrike as coming "in the form of *what appeared to be* a Hellfire missile." Appellant Br. 9 (emphasis added). And Kareem's reply brief explains that Kareem "*believed* [the third alleged airstrike] was a Hellfire missile of the type used by the United States because of its strength and the damage it caused." Reply Br. 10. At oral argument, Kareem's counsel conceded the impossibility of knowing "with any kind of certainty . . . that it was a Hellfire missile" at this stage of the litigation. . . .

Second, Kareem's factual allegations are insufficient to establish a plausible inference that the "drone launched Hellfire missile" targeted *him*, even assuming *arguendo* the United States launched the missile. . . .

. . . And the United Nations Commission of Inquiry on Syria has reported that the Syrian government "routinely targeted and killed both local and foreign journalists." These facts do not eliminate the *possibility* that the five airstrikes alleged in the complaint were attributable to the United States and specifically targeted Kareem. But they do make the necessary inferences *implausible*. [986 F.3d at 867-869.]

One fundamental pleading principle is that all reasonable inferences should be drawn in favor of the pleader. Did the Court of Appeals honor that principle? At the pleading stage — before any discovery — is there anything more that Kareem could have done to cross the line from possible to plausible?

––––––––––––––

[NSL p. 140. Insert after Note 5. For excerpt concerning framing of the Appropriations Clause from the same opinion, see *supra* insert for NSL p. 107.]

U.S. House of Representatives v. Mnuchin
United States Court of Appeals, D.C. Circuit, 2020
976 F.3d 1, *petition for cert. filed*, No. 20-1738 (U.S. June 15, 2021)

Before: MILLETT and WILKINS, Circuit Judges, and SENTELLE, Senior Circuit Judge.

SENTELLE, Senior Circuit Judge. The United States House of Representatives brought this lawsuit alleging that the Departments of Defense, Homeland Security, the Treasury, and the Interior, and the Secretaries of those departments violated the Appropriations Clause of the Constitution as well as the Administrative Procedure Act when transferring funds appropriated for other uses to finance the construction of a physical barrier along the southern border of the United States, contravening congressionally approved appropriations. The District Court for the District of Columbia held that it had no jurisdiction because the House lacked standing to challenge the defendants' actions as it did not allege a legally cognizable injury. We disagree as to the constitutional claims and therefore vacate and remand for further proceedings.

I. . . .

C. . . .

In support of its position that each chamber has a distinct interest, the House relies on statements from the founding era. In particular, the House turns to the history of the passage and amendment of the Appropriations Clause. In an early draft of the Constitution, all appropriation bills had to originate in the House and could not be altered by the Senate. *See* 2 *The Records of the Federal Convention of 1787*, at 131 (M. Farrand ed., 1911) (hereinafter *Records*); House Br. at 26-27. The origination provision was removed, the House asserts, because it made the Senate subservient to the House in appropriations and the Framers intended that each chamber would have the independent ability to limit spending. Additionally, the House references statements from the founding era that recognize the federal purse has "two strings" and "[b]oth houses must concur in untying" them. 2 *Records* at 275. The structure of the "two strings" system means, the House maintains, that the House, by not passing an appropriation, can prevent the expenditure of funds for a government project, such as the proposed border wall even if the Senate disagrees. In sum, as the House asserts, "unlike the situation in which one chamber of Congress seeks to enforce a law that it could not have enacted on its own, a suit to enforce a spending limit vindicates a decision to block or limit spending that each chamber of Congress could have effectively imposed — and, in this case, the House did impose — unilaterally." House Br. at 27-28.

II. . . .

B. . . .

. . . [*Raines v. Byrd*, 521 U.S. 811 (1997), and other Supreme Court cases] seemingly give rise to two important questions for analyzing legislative standing: First, did the defendant's action curtail the power and authority of the institution? . . .

Second, is there a mismatch between the entity pursuing litigation and the entity whose authority or right was curtailed? . . .

In addition to those two questions, our cases and the Supreme Court's additionally consider three other factors: the history of interbranch disputes in the courts, alternative political remedies available to the plaintiff, *see, e.g., Raines*, 521 U.S. at 829 (considering whether litigating the dispute is "contrary to historical experience" and whether

Congress would have "an adequate remedy" without judicial intervention), and separation of powers, *Chenoweth* [*v. Clinton*, 181 F.3d 112, 116-117 D.C. Cir. 1999)]. In none of the above decisions of the Supreme Court or this court was there ever an express determination of the first question before us: whether a single house of a bicameral legislature can ever have standing to litigate an alleged injury to its legislative prerogative distinct from the institutional standing of the entire legislature to litigate an institutional injury to the body as a whole. In [*Comm. on Judiciary of the U.S. House of Representatives v. McGahn*, 968 F.3d 755 (D.C. Cir. 2020)], the en banc court considered that question in deciding an action brought on behalf of the House of Representatives to enforce a subpoena not involving the joinder of the Senate. The court answered the standing question with a resounding "yes." . . .

When the injury alleged is to the Congress as a whole, one chamber does not have standing to litigate. When the injury is to the distinct prerogatives of a single chamber, that chamber does have standing to assert the injury. The allegations are that the Executive interfered with the prerogative of a single chamber to limit spending under the two-string theory discussed at the time of the founding. Therefore, each chamber has a distinct individual right, and in this case, one chamber has a distinct injury. That chamber has standing to bring this litigation. . . .

To put it simply, the Appropriations Clause requires two keys to unlock the Treasury, and the House holds one of those keys. The Executive Branch has, in a word, snatched the House's key out of its hands. That is the injury over which the House is suing.

That injury — the snatched key — . . . is not a generalized interest in the power to legislate. Rather, the injury is concrete and particularized to the House and the House alone. The alleged Executive Branch action cuts the House out of the appropriations process, rendering for naught its vote withholding the Executive's desired border wall funding and carefully calibrating what type of border security investments could be made. The injury, in other words, "zeroe[s] in" on the House. *Arizona State Legislature* [*v. Ariz. Indep. Redistricting Comm'n*, 576 U.S. 787, 802 (2015)]; *see also I.N.S. v. Chadha*, 462 U.S. 919, 946 (1983) ("These provisions of Art. I are integral parts of the constitutional design for the separation of powers.").

Applying the "especially rigorous" standing analysis that the Supreme Court requires in cases like this reinforces the House's injury in fact. To hold that the House is not injured or that courts cannot recognize that injury would rewrite the Appropriations Clause. That Clause has long been understood to check the power of the Executive Branch by allowing it to expend funds only as specifically authorized. As then-Judge Kavanaugh wrote for this court, the Appropriations Clause is "a bulwark of the Constitution's separation of powers among the three branches of the National Government," and it "is particularly important as a restraint on Executive Branch officers." *U.S. Dep't of Navy v. Fed. Lab. Rel. Auth.*, 665 F.3d 1339, 1347 (D.C. Cir. 2012).

The ironclad constitutional rule is that the Executive Branch cannot spend until both the House and the Senate say so. "However much money may be in the Treasury at any one time, not a dollar of it can be used in the payment of any thing not thus previously sanctioned. Any other course would give to the fiscal officers a most dangerous discretion." *Reeside v. Walker*, 52 U.S. (11 How.) at 291. The Appropriations Clause even "prevents Executive Branch officers from even inadvertently obligating the Government to pay money without statutory authority." *U.S. Dep't of Navy*, 665 F.3d at 1347 (citing *Off. Pers. Mgmt. v. Richmond*, 496 U.S. 414, 416 (1990), and *U.S. Dep't of Air Force v. Fed. Lab. Rel. Auth.*, 648 F.3d 841, 845 (D.C. Cir. 2011)).

But under the defendants' standing paradigm, the Executive Branch can freely spend Treasury funds as it wishes unless and until a veto-proof majority of both houses of Congress forbids it. Even that might not be enough: Under the defendants' standing theory, if the Executive Branch ignored that congressional override, the House would remain just as disabled to sue to protect its own institutional interests. That turns the constitutional order upside down. *Cf. Chadha*, 462 U.S. at 958 ("[T]he carefully defined limits on the power of each Branch must not be eroded."). The whole purpose of the Appropriations Clause's structural protection is to deny the Executive "an unbounded power over the public purse of the nation," and the power to "apply all its monied resources at his pleasure." *U.S. Dep't of Navy*, 665 F.3d at 1347 (quoting 3 JOSEPH STORY, COMMENTARIES ON THE CONSTITUTION OF THE UNITED STATES §1342, at 213-14 (1833)); *see also Cincinnati Soap Co. v. United States*, 301 U.S. 308, 321 (1937) (noting the Appropriations Clause "was intended as a restriction upon the disbursing authority of the Executive department").

Nor does it work to say that suit can only be brought by the House and Senate together, as that ignores the distinct power of the House alone not to untie its purse string. "[E]ach Chamber of Congress [possesses] an *ongoing* power — to veto certain Executive Branch decisions — that each House could exercise independent of any other body." [*Virginia House of Delegates v. Bethune-Hill*, 139 S. Ct. 1945, 1954 n.5 (2019)]. Unlike the affirmative power to pass legislation, the House can wield its appropriations veto fully and effectively all by itself, without any coordination with or cooperation from the Senate.

For that reason, expenditures made without the House's approval — or worse, as alleged here, in the face of its specific disapproval — cause a concrete and particularized constitutional injury that the House experiences, and can seek redress for, independently. And again, failure to recognize that injury in fact would fundamentally alter the separation of powers by allowing the Executive Branch to spend any funds the Senate is on board with, even if the House withheld its authorizations.

In short, Article III's standing requirement is meant to preserve not reorder the separation of powers. . . .

CONCLUSION

The judgment of the district court insofar as it dismisses the Administrative Procedure Act claims is affirmed. Insofar as the judgment dismisses the constitutional claims, it is vacated and remanded for further proceedings consistent with this decision.

———————

[NSL p. 151. Insert in place of the last full paragraph and the two following paragraphs on p. 152.]

Hernandez v. Mesa
United States Supreme Court, Feb. 25, 2020
140 S. Ct. 735

Justice ALITO delivered the opinion of the Court.

We are asked in this case to extend *Bivens v. Six Unknown Fed. Narcotics Agents*, 403 U.S. 388 (1971), and create a damages remedy for a cross-border shooting. As we have made clear in many prior cases, however, the Constitution's separation of powers requires us to exercise caution before extending *Bivens* to a new "context," and a claim based on a cross-border shooting arises in a context that is markedly new. Unlike any previously recognized *Bivens* claim, a cross-border shooting claim has foreign relations and national security implications. In addition, Congress has been notably hesitant to create claims based on allegedly tortious conduct abroad. Because of the distinctive characteristics of cross-border shooting claims, we refuse to extend *Bivens* into this new field.

I

The facts of this tragic case are set forth in our earlier opinion in this matter, *Hernández v. Mesa*, 582 U.S. —, 137 S. Ct. 2003 (2017) (*per curiam*). Sergio Adrián Hernández Güereca, a 15-year-old Mexican national, was with a group of friends in a concrete culvert that separates El Paso, Texas, from Ciudad Juarez, Mexico. The border runs through the center of the culvert, which was designed to hold the waters of the Rio Grande River but is now largely dry. Border Patrol Agent Jesus Mesa, Jr., detained one of Hernández's friends who had run onto the United States' side of the culvert. After Hernández, who was also on the United States' side, ran back across the culvert onto Mexican soil, Agent Mesa fired two shots at Hernández; one struck and killed him on the other side of the border. . . .

Petitioners, Hernández's parents . . . brought suit for damages in the United States District Court for the Western District of Texas. Among other claims, they sought recovery of damages under *Bivens*, alleging that Mesa violated Hernández's Fourth and Fifth Amendment rights. The District Court granted Mesa's motion to dismiss, and the Court of Appeals for the Fifth Circuit sitting en banc has twice affirmed this dismissal. . . .

We granted certiorari, 587 U.S. ——, 139 S. Ct. 2636 (2019), and now affirm.

II . . .

. . . The Constitution grants legislative power to Congress; this Court and the lower federal courts, by contrast, have only "judicial Power." Art. III, §1. But when a court recognizes an implied claim for damages on the ground that doing so furthers the "purpose" of the law, the court risks arrogating legislative power. No law "'pursues its purposes at all costs.'" *American Express Co. v. Italian Colors Restaurant*, 570 U.S. 228, 234 (2013) (quoting *Rodriguez v. United States*, 480 U.S. 522, 525-526 (1987) (*per curiam*)). Instead, lawmaking involves balancing interests and often demands compromise. Thus, a lawmaking body that enacts a provision that creates a right or prohibits specified conduct may not wish to pursue the provision's purpose to the extent of authorizing private suits for damages. For this reason, finding that a damages remedy is implied by a provision that makes no reference to that remedy may upset the careful balance of interests struck by the lawmakers.

This problem does not exist when a common-law court, which exercises a degree of lawmaking authority, fleshes out the remedies available for a common-law tort. Analogizing *Bivens* to the work of a common-law court, petitioners and some of their *amici* make much of the fact that common-law claims against federal officers for intentional torts were once available. But *Erie R. Co. v. Tompkins*, 304 U.S. 64, 78 (1938), held that "[t]here is no federal general common law," and therefore federal courts today cannot fashion new claims in the way that they could before 1938.

With the demise of federal general common law, a federal court's authority to recognize a damages remedy must rest at bottom on a statute enacted by Congress, see [*Alexander v. Sandoval*, 532 U.S. 275, 286 (2001] ("private rights of action to enforce federal law must be created by Congress"), and no statute expressly creates a *Bivens* remedy. Justice Harlan's *Bivens* concurrence argued that this power is inherent in the grant of federal question jurisdiction, see 403 U.S. at 396 (majority opinion); *id.*, at 405 (opinion of Harlan, J.), but our later cases have demanded a clearer manifestation of congressional intent, see *Abbasi*, 582 U.S., at —, 137 S. Ct., at 1856-1858.

In both statutory and constitutional cases, our watchword is caution. For example, in *Jesner v. Arab Bank, PLC*, 584 U.S. ——, —— – ——, 138 S. Ct. 1386, 1391-403 (2018) we expressed doubt about our authority to recognize any causes of action not expressly created by Congress. See also *Abbasi*, 582 U.S., at ——, 137 S. Ct., at 1856 ("If the statute does not itself so provide, a private cause of action will not be created through judicial mandate"). And we declined to recognize a claim against a foreign corporation under the Alien Tort Statute. *Jesner*, 584 U.S., at ——, 138 S. Ct., at 1408.

In constitutional cases, we have been at least equally reluctant to create new causes of action. We have recognized that Congress is best positioned to evaluate "whether, and the extent to which, monetary and other liabilities should be imposed upon individual officers and employees of the Federal Government" based on constitutional torts. [*Ziglar v. Abbasi*, 582 U.S. ——, 137 S. Ct. 1843 (2017)], at 1856. We have stated that expansion of *Bivens* is "a 'disfavored' judicial activity," 582 U.S., at ——, 137 S. Ct., at 1857 (quoting *Ashcroft v. Iqbal*, 556 U.S. 662, 675 (2009)), and have gone so far as to observe that if "the Court's three *Bivens* cases [had] been . . . decided today," it is doubtful that we would have reached the same result, 582 U.S., at ——, 137 S. Ct., at 1856. And for almost 40 years, we have consistently rebuffed requests to add to the claims allowed under *Bivens*.

When asked to extend *Bivens*, we engage in a two-step inquiry. We first inquire whether the request involves a claim that arises in a "new context" or involves a "new category of defendants." [*Correctional*

Services Corp. v. Malesko, 534 U.S. 61, 68 (2001)]. And our understanding of a "new context" is broad. We regard a context as "new" if it is "different in a meaningful way from previous *Bivens* cases decided by this Court." *Abbasi*, 582 U.S., at ——, 137 S. Ct., at 1859.

When we find that a claim arises in a new context, we proceed to the second step and ask whether there are any """"special factors [that] counse[l] hesitation"""" about granting the extension. *Id.*, at ——, 137 S. Ct., at 1857 (quoting *Carlson* [v. Green, 446 U.S. 14 (1980)], at 18, in turn quoting *Bivens*, 403 U.S. at 396). If there are — that is, if we have reason to pause before applying *Bivens* in a new context or to a new class of defendants — we reject the request.

We have not attempted to "create an exhaustive list" of factors that may provide a reason not to extend *Bivens*, but we have explained that "central to [this] analysis" are "separation-of-powers principles." *Abbasi*, 582 U.S., at ——, 137 S. Ct., at 1857. We thus consider the risk of interfering with the authority of the other branches, and we ask whether "there are sound reasons to think Congress might doubt the efficacy or necessity of a damages remedy," *id.*, at ——, 137 S. Ct., at 1858, and "whether the Judiciary is well suited, absent congressional action or instruction, to consider and weigh the costs and benefits of allowing a damages action to proceed," *id.*, at ——, 137 S. Ct., at 1858.

III

A

The *Bivens* claims in this case assuredly arise in a new context. Petitioners contend that their Fourth and Fifth Amendment claims do not involve a new context because *Bivens* and *Davis* [v. *Passman*, 442 U.S. 228 (1979),] involved claims under those same two amendments, but that argument rests on a basic misunderstanding of what our cases mean by a new context. A claim may arise in a new context even if it is based on the same constitutional provision as a claim in a case in which a damages remedy was previously recognized. And once we look beyond the constitutional provisions invoked in *Bivens*, *Davis*, and the present case, it is glaringly obvious that petitioners' claims involve a new context, *i.e.*, one that is meaningfully different. *Bivens* concerned an allegedly unconstitutional arrest and search carried out in New York City, 403 U.S. at 389; *Davis* concerned alleged sex discrimination on Capitol Hill, 442 U.S. at 230. There is a world of difference between those claims and petitioners' cross-border shooting claims, where "the risk of disruptive

intrusion by the Judiciary into the functioning of other branches" is
significant. *Abbasi*, 582 U.S., at ——, 137 S. Ct., at 1860.

Because petitioners assert claims that arise in a new context, we must
proceed to the next step and ask whether there are factors that counsel
hesitation. As we will explain, there are multiple, related factors that
raise warning flags.

B

The first is the potential effect on foreign relations. "The political
branches, not the Judiciary, have the responsibility and institutional
capacity to weigh foreign-policy concerns." *Jesner*, 584 U.S., at ——,
138 S. Ct., at 1403. Indeed, we have said that "matters relating 'to the
conduct of foreign relations . . . are so exclusively entrusted to the
political branches of government as to be largely immune from judicial
inquiry or interference.'" *Haig v. Agee*, 453 U.S. 280, 292 (1981)
(quoting *Harisiades v. Shaughnessy*, 342 U.S. 580, 589 (1952)). "Thus,
unless Congress specifically has provided otherwise, courts traditionally
have been reluctant to intrude upon the authority of the Executive in
[these matters]." *Department of Navy v. Egan*, 484 U.S. 518, 530 (1988).
We must therefore be especially wary before allowing a *Bivens* remedy
that impinges on this arena.

A cross-border shooting is by definition an international incident; it
involves an event that occurs simultaneously in two countries and affects
both countries' interests. Such an incident may lead to a disagreement
between those countries, as happened in this case.

The United States, through the Executive Branch, which has "'the
lead role in foreign policy,'" *Medellín v. Texas*, 552 U.S. 491, 524 (2008)
(alteration omitted), has taken the position that this incident should be
handled in a particular way — namely, that Agent Mesa should not face
charges in the United States nor be extradited to stand trial in Mexico. As
noted, the Executive decided not to take action against Agent Mesa
because it found that he "did not act inconsistently with [Border Patrol]
policy or training regarding use of force." DOJ Press Release. We
presume that Border Patrol policy and training incorporate both the
Executive's understanding of the Fourth Amendment's prohibition of
unreasonable seizures and the Executive's assessment of circumstances
at the border. Thus, the Executive judged Agent Mesa's conduct by what
it regards as reasonable conduct by an agent under the circumstances that
Mesa faced at the time of the shooting, and based on the application of
those standards, it declined to prosecute. The Executive does not want a
Mexican criminal court to judge Agent Mesa's conduct by whatever

standards would be applicable under Mexican law; nor does it want a jury in a *Bivens* action to apply its own understanding of what constituted reasonable conduct by a Border Patrol agent under the circumstances of this case. Such a jury determination, the Executive claims, would risk the """"embarrassment of our government abroad" through "multifarious pronouncements by various departments on one question.""""" Brief for United States as *Amicus Curiae* 18 (quoting *Sanchez-Espinoza v. Reagan*, 770 F.2d 202, 209 (C.A.D.C. 1985) (Scalia, J.)).

The Government of Mexico has taken a different view of what should be done. It has requested that Agent Mesa be extradited for criminal prosecution in a Mexican court under Mexican law, and it has supported petitioners' *Bivens* suit. In a brief filed in this Court, Mexico suggests that shootings by Border Patrol agents are a persistent problem and argues that the United States has an obligation under international law, specifically Article 6(1) of the International Covenant on Civil and Political Rights, Dec. 19, 1966, S. Treaty Doc. No. 95-20, 999 U.N.T.S. 174, to provide a remedy for the shooting in this case. Mexico states that it "has a responsibility to look after the well-being of its nationals" and that "it is a priority to Mexico to see that the United States provides adequate means to hold the agents accountable and to compensate the victims."

Both the United States and Mexico have legitimate and important interests that may be affected by the way in which this matter is handled. The United States has an interest in ensuring that agents assigned the difficult and important task of policing the border are held to standards and judged by procedures that satisfy United States law and do not undermine the agents' effectiveness and morale. Mexico has an interest in exercising sovereignty over its territory and in protecting and obtaining justice for its nationals. It is not our task to arbitrate between them.

In the absence of judicial intervention, the United States and Mexico would attempt to reconcile their interests through diplomacy — and that has occurred. The broad issue of violence along the border, the occurrence of crossborder shootings, and this particular matter have been addressed through diplomatic channels. In 2014, Mexico and the United States established a joint Border Violence Prevention Council, and the two countries have addressed cross-border shootings through the United States-Mexico bilateral Human Rights Dialogue. Following the Justice Department investigation in the present case, the United States reaffirmed its commitment to "work with the Mexican government within existing mechanisms and agreements to prevent future incidents." DOJ Press Release.

For these reasons, petitioners' assertion that their claims have "nothing to do with the substance or conduct of U.S. foreign . . . policy," is plainly wrong.

C

Petitioners are similarly incorrect in deprecating the Fifth Circuit's conclusion that the issue here implicates an element of national security.

One of the ways in which the Executive protects this country is by attempting to control the movement of people and goods across the border, and that is a daunting task. The United States' border with Mexico extends for 1,900 miles, and every day thousands of persons and a large volume of goods enter this country at ports of entry on the southern border. The lawful passage of people and goods in both directions across the border is beneficial to both countries.

Unfortunately, there is also a large volume of illegal cross-border traffic. During the last fiscal year, approximately 850,000 persons were apprehended attempting to enter the United States illegally from Mexico, and large quantities of drugs were smuggled across the border. In addition, powerful criminal organizations operating on both sides of the border present a serious law enforcement problem for both countries.

On the United States' side, the responsibility for attempting to prevent the illegal entry of dangerous persons and goods rests primarily with the U.S. Customs and Border Protection Agency, and one of its main responsibilities is to "detect, respond to, and interdict terrorists, drug smugglers and traffickers, human smugglers and traffickers, and other persons who may undermine the security of the United States." 6 U.S.C. §211(c)(5). While Border Patrol agents often work miles from the border, some, like Agent Mesa, are stationed right at the border and have the responsibility of attempting to prevent illegal entry. For these reasons, the conduct of agents positioned at the border has a clear and strong connection to national security, as the Fifth Circuit understood. 885 F.3d at 819.

Petitioners protest that "'shooting people who are just walking down a street in Mexico'" does not involve national security, but that misses the point. The question is not whether national security requires such conduct — of course, it does not—but whether the Judiciary should alter the framework established by the political branches for addressing cases in which it is alleged that lethal force was unlawfully employed by an agent at the border. Cf. *Abbasi*, 582 U.S., at ——, 137 S. Ct., at 1861 (explaining that "[n]ational-security policy is the prerogative of the Congress and President").

We have declined to extend *Bivens* where doing so would interfere with the system of military discipline created by statute and regulation, and a similar consideration is applicable here. Since regulating the conduct of agents at the border unquestionably has national security implications, the risk of undermining border security provides reason to hesitate before extending *Bivens* into this field. See *Abbasi*, 582 U.S., at ——, 137 S. Ct., at 1861 ("Judicial inquiry into the national-security realm raises 'concerns for the separation of powers'" (quoting *Christopher v. Harbury*, 536 U.S. 403, 417 (2002))).

D

Our reluctance to take that step is reinforced by our survey of what Congress has done in statutes addressing related matters. We frequently "loo[k] to analogous statutes for guidance on the appropriate boundaries of judgemade causes of action." *Jesner*, 584 U.S., at ——, 138 S. Ct., at 1403 (opinion of Kennedy, J.). When foreign relations are implicated, it "is even more important . . . 'to look for legislative guidance before exercising innovative authority over substantive law.'" *Id.*, at ——, 138 S. Ct., at 1403 (quoting *Sosa v. Alvarez-Machain*, 542 U.S. 692, 726 (2004)). Accordingly, it is "telling," *Abbasi*, 582 U.S., at ——, 137 S. Ct., at 1862, that Congress has repeatedly declined to authorize the award of damages for injury inflicted outside our borders.

A leading example is 42 U.S.C. §1983, which permits the recovery of damages for constitutional violations by officers acting under color of *state* law. We have described *Bivens* as a "more limited" "federal analog" to §1983. *Hartman v. Moore*, 547 U.S. 250, 254, n. 2 (2006). It is therefore instructive that Congress chose to make §1983 available only to "citizen[s] of the United States or other person[s] within the jurisdiction thereof." It would be "anomalous to impute . . . a judicially implied cause of action beyond the bounds [Congress has] delineated for [a] comparable express caus[e] of action." *Blue Chip Stamps v. Manor Drug Stores*, 421 U.S. 723, 736 (1975). Thus, the limited scope of §1983 weighs against recognition of the *Bivens* claim at issue here.

Section 1983's express limitation to the claims brought by citizens and persons subject to United States jurisdiction is especially significant, but even if this explicit limitation were lacking, we would presume that §1983 did not apply abroad. See *RJR Nabisco, Inc. v. European Community*, 579 U.S. ——, ——, 136 S. Ct. 2090, 2100 (2016) ("Absent clearly expressed congressional intent to the contrary, federal laws will be construed to have only domestic application"). We presume that statutes do not apply extraterritorially to "ensure that the Judiciary does not erroneously adopt an interpretation of U.S. law that carries foreign policy consequences not clearly intended by the political branches." *Kiobel v. Royal Dutch Petroleum Co.*, 569 U.S. 108 (2013); see also *EEOC v. Arabian American Oil Co.*, 499 U.S. 244, 248 (1991).

If this danger provides a reason for caution when Congress has enacted a statute but has not provided expressly whether it applies abroad, we have even greater reason for hesitation in deciding whether to extend a judge-made cause of action beyond our borders. "[T]he danger of unwarranted judicial interference in the conduct of foreign policy is magnified" where "the question is not what Congress has done but instead what courts may do." *Kiobel*, 569 U.S. at 116. Where Congress has not spoken at all, the likelihood of impinging on its foreign affairs authority is especially acute. . . .

. . . When Congress has enacted statutes creating a damages remedy for persons injured by United States Government officers, it has taken care to preclude claims for injuries that occurred abroad.

Instead, when Congress has provided compensation for injuries suffered by aliens outside the United States, it has done so by empowering Executive Branch officials to make payments under circumstances found to be appropriate. . . .

This pattern of congressional action — refraining from authorizing damages actions for injury inflicted abroad by Government officers, while providing alternative avenues for compensation in some situations — gives us further reason to hesitate about extending *Bivens* in this case.

E

In sum, this case features multiple factors that counsel hesitation about extending *Bivens,* but they can all be condensed to one concern — respect for the separation of powers. . . .

Congress's decision not to provide a judicial remedy does not compel us to step into its shoes. "The absence of statutory relief for a constitutional violation . . . does not by any means necessarily imply that courts should award money damages against the officers responsible for the violation." *Schweiker* [*v. Chilicky*, 487 U.S. 412 (1988)], at 421-422; see also [*United States v. Stanley*, 483 U.S. 669 (1987)], at 683 ("[I]t is irrelevant to a 'special factors' analysis whether the laws currently on the books afford [plaintiff] an 'adequate' federal remedy for his injuries").

When evaluating whether to extend *Bivens,* the most important question "is 'who should decide' whether to provide for a damages remedy, Congress or the courts?" *Abbasi*, 582 U.S., at ——, 137 S. Ct., at 1857 (quoting *Bush* [*v. Lucas*, 462 U.S. 367 (1983)], at 380. The correct "answer most often will be Congress." 582 U.S., at ——, 137 S. Ct., at 1857. That is undoubtedly the answer here.

* * *

The judgment of the United States Court of Appeals for the Fifth Circuit is affirmed.

It is so ordered.

Justice THOMAS, with whom Justice GORSUCH joins, concurring. The Court correctly applies our precedents to conclude that the implied cause of action created in *Bivens v. Six Unknown Fed. Narcotics Agents*, 403 U.S. 388 (1971), should not be extended to cross-border shootings. I therefore join its opinion.

I write separately because, in my view, the time has come to consider discarding the *Bivens* doctrine altogether. The foundation for *Bivens* — the practice of creating implied causes of action in the statutory context — has already been abandoned. And the Court has consistently refused to extend the *Bivens* doctrine for nearly 40 years, even going so far as to suggest that *Bivens* and its progeny were wrongly decided. *Stare decisis* provides no "veneer of respectability to our continued application of [these] demonstrably incorrect precedents." *Gamble v. United States*, 587 U.S. ——, ——, 139 S. Ct. 1960, 1981 (2019) (Thomas, J., concurring). To ensure that we are not "perpetuat[ing] a usurpation of the legislative power," *id.*, at ——, 139 S. Ct., at 1984, we should reevaluate our continued recognition of even a limited form of the *Bivens* doctrine. . . .

The Court's method of implying causes of action for damages in the statutory context provided the foundation for the approach taken in *Bivens*. Therefore, as the Court backed away from creating statutory causes of action, it also effectively cabined the *Bivens* doctrine to the facts of *Bivens*, *Davis*, and *Carlson*. For nearly 40 years, the Court has "'consistently refused to extend *Bivens* liability to any new context or new category of defendants.'" *Abbasi*, 582 U.S., at ——, 137 S. Ct., at 1857 (quoting *Malesko*, 534 U.S. at 68).

In doing so, our decisions have undermined the validity of the *Bivens* doctrine. As the Court recognizes, "[w]e have stated that expansion of *Bivens* is a disfavored judicial activity." And we have now repeatedly acknowledged the shaky foundation on which *Bivens* rests, stating that "in light of the changes to the Court's general approach to recognizing implied damages remedies, it is possible that the analysis in the Court's three *Bivens* cases might have been different if they were decided today."

Abbasi, 582 U.S., at ——, 137 S. Ct., at 1856; see also *ante*, at 743 (noting that it is "doubtful that we would have reached the same result" if *Bivens* were decided today). Thus, it appears that we have already repudiated the foundation of the *Bivens* doctrine; nothing is left to do but overrule it.

Our continued adherence to even a limited form of the *Bivens* doctrine appears to "perpetuat[e] a usurpation of the legislative power." *Gamble*, 587 U.S., at ——, 139 S. Ct., at 1984 (Thomas, J., concurring). Federal courts lack the authority to engage in the distinctly legislative task of creating causes of action for damages to enforce federal positive law. We have clearly recognized as much in the statutory context. I see no reason for us to take a different approach if the right asserted to recover damages derives from the Constitution, rather than from a federal statute. Either way, we are exercising legislative power vested in Congress. Cf. *Carlson*, 446 U.S. at 51 (Rehnquist, J., dissenting) ("The policy questions at issue in the creation of any tort remedies, constitutional or otherwise, involve judgments as to diverse factors that are more appropriately made by the legislature than by this Court in an attempt to fashion a constitutional common law"). . . .

Justice GINSBURG, with whom Justice BREYER, Justice SOTOMAYOR, and Justice KAGAN join, dissenting. . . . Rogue U.S. officer conduct falls within a familiar, not a "new," *Bivens* setting. Even if the setting could be characterized as "new," plaintiffs lack recourse to alternative remedies, and no "special factors" counsel against a *Bivens* remedy. Neither U.S. foreign policy nor national security is in fact endangered by the litigation. Moreover, concerns attending the application of our law to conduct occurring abroad are not involved, for plaintiffs seek the application of U.S. law to conduct occurring inside our borders. I would therefore hold that the plaintiffs' complaint crosses the *Bivens* threshold. . . .

III

Plaintiffs' *Bivens* action arises in a setting kin to *Bivens* itself: Mesa, plaintiffs allege, acted in disregard of instructions governing his conduct and of Hernández's constitutional rights. *Abbasi* acknowledged the "fixed principle" that plaintiffs may bring *Bivens* suits against federal law enforcement officers for "seizure[s]" that violate the Fourth Amendment. 582 U.S., at ——, 137 S. Ct., at 1877. Using lethal force against a person who "poses no immediate threat to the officer and no threat to others" surely qualifies as an unreasonable seizure. *Tennessee v.*

Garner, 471 U.S. 1, 11 (1985). The complaint states that Mesa engaged in that very conduct; it alleged, specifically, that Hernández was unarmed and posed no threat to Mesa or others. For these reasons, as Mesa acknowledged at oral argument, Hernández's parents could have maintained a *Bivens* action had the bullet hit Hernández while he was running up or down the United States side of the embankment.

The only salient difference here: the fortuity that the bullet happened to strike Hernández on the Mexican side of the embankment. But Hernández's location at the precise moment the bullet landed should not matter one whit. After all, "[t]he purpose of *Bivens* is to deter the *officer*." *Abbasi*, 582 U.S., at ——, 137 S. Ct., at 1860 (internal quotation marks omitted). And primary conduct constrained by the Fourth Amendment is an *officer*'s unjustified resort to excessive force. Mesa's allegedly unwarranted deployment of deadly force occurred on United States soil. It scarcely makes sense for a remedy trained on deterring rogue officer conduct to turn upon a happenstance subsequent to the conduct — a bullet landing in one half of a culvert, not the other.

Nor would it make sense to deem some culvert locations "new settings" for *Bivens* purposes, but others (those inside the United States), familiar territory. As recounted in Justice Breyer's dissent earlier in this litigation, the culvert "does not itself contain any physical features of a border"; it consists of wide swaths of "concrete-lined empty space" with fencing on each side. *Hernández*, 582 U.S., at ——, 137 S. Ct., at 2009. See also *id.*, at ——, 137 S. Ct., at 2006-2007 (noting "the near irrelevance of [the] midculvert line . . . for most border-related purposes"). It is not asserted that Mesa "knew on which side of the boundary line [his] bullet would land." *Id.*, at ——, 137 S. Ct., at 2010.

Finally, although the bullet happened to land on the Mexican side of the culvert, the United States, as in *Bivens*, unquestionably has jurisdiction to prescribe law governing a Border Patrol agent's conduct. That prescriptive jurisdiction reaches "conduct that . . . takes place within [United States] territory." Restatement (Third) of Foreign Relations Law of the United States §402 (1986). The place of a rogue officer's conduct "has peculiar significance" to choice of the applicable law where, as here, "the primary purpose of the tort rule involved is to deter or punish misconduct." Restatement (Second) of Conflict of Laws §145, Comment *e*, p. 420 (1969).

IV

Even accepting, *arguendo*, that the setting in this case could be characterized as "new," there is still no good reason why Hernández's parents should face a closed courtroom door. As in *Bivens*, plaintiffs lack recourse to alternative remedies. And not one of the "special factors" the Court identifies weigh[s] any differently based on where a bullet happens to land. . . .

B

The special factors featured by the Court relate, in the main, to foreign policy and national security. But, as suggested earlier, no policies or policymakers are challenged in this case. Plaintiffs target the rogue actions of a rank-and-file law enforcement officer acting in violation of rules controlling his office. See 8 CFR §287.8(a)(2)(ii) (2019) (limiting use of deadly force). The situation here presented resembles cases *Abbasi* distinguished — cases involving "individual instances of . . . law enforcement overreach." 582 U.S., at ——, 137 S. Ct., at 1862.

The Court nevertheless asserts that the instant suit has a "potential effect on foreign relations" because it invites courts "to arbitrate between" the United States and Mexico. *Ante*, at 744, 745. Plaintiffs, however, have brought a civil damages action, no different from one a federal court would entertain had the fatal shot hit Hernández before he reached the Mexican side of the border. True, cross-border shootings spark bilateral discussion, but so too does a range of smuggling and other border-related issues that courts routinely address "concurrently with whatever diplomacy may also be addressing them." *Rodriguez v. Swartz*, 899 F.3d 719, 747 (C.A.9 2018). The Government has identified no deleterious effect on diplomatic negotiations in any case after the Ninth Circuit held that the mother of a boy killed in a cross-border shooting could institute a *Bivens* action. See 899 F.3d at 734.

Moreover, the Court, in this case, cannot escape a "potential effect on foreign relations," by declining to recognize a *Bivens* action. As the Mexican Government alerted the Court: "[R]efus[al] to consider [Hernández's] parents' claim on the merits . . . is what has the potential to negatively affect international relations."

Notably, recognizing a *Bivens* suit here honors our Nation's international commitments. Article 9(5) of the International Covenant on Civil and Political Rights (ICCPR), Dec. 19, 1966, S. Treaty Doc. No. 95-20, 999 U.N. T. S. 176, provides that "[a]nyone who has been the victim of unlawful arrest or detention shall have an enforceable right to compensation." The United States ratified the ICCPR with the "understandin[g]" that Article 9(5) "require[s] the provision of effective and enforceable mechanisms by which a victim of an unlawful arrest or detention or a miscarriage of justice may seek and, where justified, obtain compensation from either the responsible individual or the appropriate governmental entity." U.S. Reservations, Declarations, and Understandings, ICCPR, 138 Cong. Rec. 8071 (1992). See also 1676 U. N. T. S. 544 (entered into force Sept. 8, 1992). One fitting mechanism to obtain compensation is a *Bivens* action. See Senate Committee on Foreign Relations, ICCPR, S. Exec. Rep. No. 102-23, p. 15 (1992).

The Court also asserts, as cause for hesitation, "the risk of undermining border security." But the Court speaks with generality of the national-security involvement of Border Patrol officers. It does not home in on how a *Bivens* suit for an unjustified killing would in fact undermine security at the border. *Abbasi* cautioned against invocations of national security of this very order: "[N]ational-security concerns must not become a talisman used to ward off inconvenient claims — a 'label' used to 'cover a multitude of sins.'" 582 U.S., at —, 137 S. Ct., at 1862 (quoting *Mitchell v. Forsyth*, 472 U.S. 511, 523 (1985)). Instructions regulating Border Patrol agents tell them to guard against deploying unjustified deadly force. See 8 CFR §287.8(a)(2)(ii). Given that instruction, I do not grasp how allowing a *Bivens* action here would intrude upon the political branches' national-security prerogatives. . . .

Nor are concerns sometimes attending application of our law abroad implicated in this case. True, the Court has applied a "presumption against extraterritorial application" to statutes that do not make plain their governance beyond U.S. borders. *Kiobel v. Royal Dutch Petroleum Co.*, 569 U.S. 108, 115 (2013). But plaintiffs in this case allege a tort stemming from stateside conduct. Cf. *id.*, at 124-125, 133 S. Ct. 1659 (if conduct at issue "touch[es] and concern[s] the territory of the United States . . . with sufficient force," the presumption against extraterritoriality is displaced). This case scarcely resembles those in which applying "U.S. law . . . to conduct in foreign countries" might spark "international discord." *RJR Nabisco, Inc. v. European Community*, 579 U.S. —, —, 136 S. Ct. 2090, 2100 (2016). Quite the opposite. Withholding a *Bivens* suit here threatens to exacerbate bilateral relations, and in no way fosters our international commitments.

V

. . . [A]*mici* warn that, "[w]ithout the possibility of civil liability, the unlikely prospect of discipline or criminal prosecution will not provide a meaningful deterrent to abuse at the border." In short, it is all too apparent that to redress injuries like the one suffered here, it is *Bivens* or nothing.

* * *

I resist the conclusion that "nothing" is the answer required in this case. I would reverse the Fifth Circuit's judgment and hold that plaintiffs can sue Mesa in federal court for violating their son's Fourth and Fifth Amendment rights.

[NSL p. 227. Insert at the end of Note 1.]

The Supreme Court reversed *Hernandez II* without reaching the question of extraterritoriality, holding that the plaintiffs had no implied *Bivens* cause of action. *Hernandez v. Mesa*, 140 S. Ct. 735 (2020). See insert for Chapter 5, *supra* p. 151.

[NSL p. 228. Insert at the end of Note 4.]

In *Hernandez v. Mesa*, 140 S. Ct. 735 (2020) (see insert for Chapter 5, *supra* p. 151), the Supreme Court declined to find an implied cause of action for the plaintiffs under *Bivens*. It then vacated and remanded *Rodriguez* in light of *Hernandez*. *Swartz v. Rodriguez*, 140 S. Ct. 1258 (2020) (mem.).

[NSL p. 228. Insert new Note 5.]

5. *Do Foreigners Abroad Have Any Constitutional Rights?* In *Hernandez II*, the Supreme Court failed to directly address the question whether noncitizens located outside the United States had any rights under the U.S. Constitution (assuming without deciding that the Petitioners in that case did). But in another decision later in the same year, the Court came closer to providing an answer.

In *Agency for International Development v. Alliance for Open Society International, Inc.*, 140 S. Ct. 2082 (2020), the plaintiffs asserted that their foreign affiliates located abroad had a constitutional right under the First Amendment to challenge a U.S. policy.

The Court, in an opinion by Justice Kavanaugh, rejected their claim:

> Plaintiffs' position runs headlong into two bedrock principles of American law.
>
> *First*, it is long settled as a matter of American constitutional law that foreign citizens outside U.S. territory do not possess rights under

the U. S. Constitution. . . . [citing, *inter alia*, *United States v. Verdugo-Urquidez*, 494 U.S. 259, 265-275 (1990), *Johnson v. Eisentrager*, 339 U.S. 763, 784 (1950), and U.S. Const., Preamble.]

As the Court has recognized, foreign citizens *in the United States* may enjoy certain constitutional rights — to take just one example, the right to due process in a criminal trial. See, *e.g.*, *Verdugo-Urquidez*, 494 U.S. at 270-271. And so too, the Court has ruled that, under some circumstances, foreign citizens in the U.S. Territories — or in "a territory" under the "indefinite" and "complete and total control" and "within the constant jurisdiction" of the United States — may possess certain constitutional rights. *Boumediene* [*v. Bush*, 553 U.S. 723, 755-771 (2008) (casebook p. 850)]. But the Court has not allowed foreign citizens outside the United States or such U.S. territory to assert rights under the U.S. Constitution. If the rule were otherwise, actions by American military, intelligence, and law enforcement personnel against foreign organizations or foreign citizens in foreign countries would be constrained by the foreign citizens' purported rights under the U.S. Constitution. That has never been the law. See *Verdugo-Urquidez*, 494 U.S. at 273-274; *Eisentrager*, 339 U.S. at 784. . . . [140 S. Ct. at 2086-2087.]

Dissenting, Justice Breyer, joined by Justices Ginsburg and Sotomayor (Justice Kagan did not participate), disputed the existence of any such "bedrock principle":

The idea that foreign citizens abroad *never* have constitutional rights is not a "bedrock" legal principle. At most, one might say that they are unlikely to enjoy very often extraterritorial protection under the Constitution. Or one might say that the matter is undecided. But this Court has studiously avoided establishing an absolute rule that forecloses that protection in all circumstances. . . .

. . . The exhaustive review of our precedents that we conducted in *Boumediene v. Bush*, 553 U.S. 723 (2008), pointed to the opposite conclusion. In *Boumediene*, we rejected the Government's argument that our decision in *Johnson v. Eisentrager*, 339 U.S. 7635 (1950), "adopted a formalistic" test "for determining the reach" of constitutional protection to foreign citizens on foreign soil. 553 U.S. at 762. This is to say, we rejected the position that the majority propounds today. Its "constricted reading" of *Eisentrager* and our other precedents is not the law.

The law, we confirmed in *Boumediene*, is that constitutional "questions of extraterritoriality turn on objective factors and practical concerns" present in a given case, "not formalism" of the sort the majority invokes today. 553 U.S. at 764. Those considerations include the extent of *de facto* U.S. Government control (if any) over foreign territory. But they also include the nature of the constitutional protection sought, how feasible extending it would be in a given case, and the foreign citizen's status vis-à-vis the United States, among other pertinent circumstances that might arise. 553 U.S. at 766; see also *United States v. Verdugo-Urquidez*, 494 U.S. 259, 278 (Kennedy, J., concurring) (providing the decisive fifth vote for rejecting a foreign citizen's claim to constitutional protection on foreign soil outside U.S. control because "[t]he conditions and considerations of *this case* would make adherence to *the Fourth Amendment's warrant requirement* impracticable and anomalous" (emphasis added)). Our precedents reject absolutism. . . .

There is wisdom in our past restraint. Situations where a foreign citizen outside U.S. Territory might fairly assert constitutional rights are not difficult to imagine. Long-term permanent residents are "foreign citizens." Does the Constitution therefore allow American officials to assault them at will while "outside U.S. territory"? Many international students attend college in the United States. Does the First Amendment permit a public university to revoke their admission based on an unpopular political stance they took on social media while home for the summer? Foreign citizens who have never set foot in the United States, for that matter, often protest when Presidents travel overseas. Does that mean Secret Service agents can, consistent with our Constitution, seriously injure peaceful protestors abroad without any justification?

We have never purported to give a single "bedrock" answer to these or myriad other extraterritoriality questions that might arise in the future. To purport to do so today, in a case where the question is not presented and where the matter is not briefed, is in my view a serious mistake. [140 S. Ct. at 2099-2100 (Breyer, J., dissenting).]

Which reading is more consistent with *Verdugo-Urquidez*? If the Court's "no rights" principle was not bedrock before *Agency for International Development*, is it bedrock after?

[NSL p. 237. Insert at end of Note 5.]

In *Nestlé USA, Inc. v. Doe*, 141 S. Ct. 1931 (2021), the Supreme Court nearly slammed the door on ATS claims against U.S. corporations as well. Plaintiffs claimed that the defendant aided and abetted the use of child slaves to harvest cocoa in the Ivory Coast. Nestlé USA was alleged to have made key financial and operational decisions in the United States sufficient to provide the touch-and-concern nexus, although the child slavery took place entirely in the Ivory Coast.

Not good enough, the Court held 8-1. "[A]llegations of general corporate activity — like decisionmaking — cannot alone establish domestic application of the ATS. . . . To plead facts sufficient to support a domestic application of the ATS, plaintiffs must allege more domestic conduct than general corporate activity." *Id.* at 1937. The Court reiterated its stiff test for extraterritorial applications of the ATS:

> Our precedents "reflect a two-step framework for analyzing extraterritoriality issues." *RJR Nabisco, Inc. v. European Community*, 579 U.S. 325, 337 (2016). First, we presume that a statute applies only domestically, and we ask "whether the statute gives a clear, affirmative indication" that rebuts this presumption. *Ibid.* For the ATS, *Kiobel* answered that question in the negative. 569 U.S. at 124. Although we have interpreted its purely jurisdictional text to implicitly enable courts to create causes of action, the ATS does not expressly "regulate conduct" at all, much less "evince a 'clear indication of extraterritoriality.'" *Id.*, at 115-118. Courts thus cannot give "extraterritorial reach" to any cause of action judicially created under the ATS. *Id.*, at 117-118. Second, where the statute, as here, does not apply extraterritorially, plaintiffs must establish that "the conduct relevant to the statute's focus occurred in the United States." *RJR Nabisco*, 579 U.S., at 337. "[T]hen the case involves a permissible domestic application even if other conduct occurred abroad." *Ibid.* [141 S. Ct. at 1936.]

See generally William S. Dodge, *The Surprisingly Broad Implications of Nestlé USA Inc. v. Doe for Human Rights Litigation and Extraterritoriality*, Just Security, June 18, 2021 (arguing that emphasis on intraterritorial conduct relevant to statute's focus may bar ATS cases against natural persons as well as most U.S. corporations, and could affect extraterritoriality analysis in other unforeseen contexts).

Justices Thomas, Kavanaugh, and Gorsuch, however, would have gone further. Emphasizing that no court since *Sosa v. Alvarez-Machain*, 542 U.S. 692 (2004) (noted at NSL p. 203), has recognized a new cause of action under the ATS (beyond the three historical torts identified in *Sosa*), they were prepared to say that *no court should. See* 141 S. Ct. at 1937–40; *id.* at 1940–43 (Gorsuch, J., concurring). Creating new causes of action, especially on behalf of foreign plaintiffs or against foreign defendants, they asserted, is the business of Congress, not the courts.

But, Justices Sotomayor, Breyer, and Kagan responded, the First Congress *already* did that business when it "made the legislative determination that a remedy should be available under the ATS to foreign citizens who suffer 'tort[s] . . . in violation of the law of nations.' 28 U.S.C. §1350. Barring some extraordinary collateral consequence that could not have been foreseen by Congress, they claimed, federal courts should not, under the guise of judicial discretion, second-guess that legislative decision." 141 S. Ct. at 1946 (Sotomayor, J., concurring in part and concurring in the judgment) (alteration in original).

[NSL p. 262. Add to Note 12.]

In early 2020, the ICC reversed itself, ruling that the investigation could go forward. *See* Susannah George, *International Court Approves Investigation into Possible War Crimes in Afghanistan Involving U.S. Troops*, Wash. Post, Mar. 5, 2020. Secretary of State Mike Pompeo called the Court's move "a truly breathtaking action by an unaccountable political institution masquerading as a legal body." *Id.* Was he right?

In response, President Trump declared a national emergency and invoked the IEEPA to block the property of any foreign person determined by the Secretary of State to have "directly engaged in any effort by the ICC to investigate, arrest, detain, or prosecute any United States personnel without the consent of the United States," and to bar their entry into the United States. Exec. Order No. 13,928, *Executive Order on Blocking Property of Certain Persons Associated With The International Criminal Court* §1(a)(i)(A), 85 Fed. Reg. 36,139, 36,139 (June 11, 2020). That executive order was revoked by President Biden. Pranshu Verma & Marlise Simons, *Reversing Trump, Biden Repeals Sanctions on Human Rights Prosecutor*, N.Y. Times, Apr. 2, 2021.

[NSL p. 285, CTL p. 123. Insert after Note 2.]

2.1. Universal Jurisdiction for War Crimes? To the extent that domestic criminal laws and the limited reach of the ICC fail to fully remediate war crimes, might the concept of universal jurisdiction lead to the emergence of customary international law justice for victims? Universal jurisdiction rests on the assumption that some crimes are so widely regarded as heinous that their perpetrators are subject to prosecution in every nation, no matter when, where, or against whom those crimes were committed. Included are crimes against humanity, war crimes, genocide, and torture. See NSL p. 1079, CTL p. 731, Note 6. For example, in 2021 a German court convicted a former Syrian secret police officer of aiding and abetting crimes against humanity for his role nearly a decade earlier in arresting and transporting protesters to an interrogation center known for torture. Other prosecutions for atrocities committed in Syria, Liberia, and other countries have occurred in France, Switzerland, Finland, and elsewhere, mostly in Europe. Rick Gladstone,

An Old Legal Doctrine That Puts War Criminals in the Reach of Justice, N.Y. Times, Feb. 28, 2021.

Infamous cases based on universal jurisdiction include Israel's prosecution of Adolf Eichmann, the former Nazi SS officer who oversaw the transport of Jews to Holocaust death camps. After living quietly in Argentina for years, Eichmann was captured by Israeli security personnel in 1960, then taken to Israel, convicted by an Israeli court, and executed in 1962. Former Chilean dictator Augusto Pinochet was arrested in Britain pursuant to a Spanish arrest warrant in 1998, based on Spain's assertion of universal jurisdiction to try Pinochet for human rights atrocities during his 17-year rule. British courts refused to block his extradition to Spain, although for medical reasons Pinochet was later found incapable of standing trial.

While theories of universal jurisdiction have not been widely accepted in U.S. courts, lawyers have creatively used other theories of jurisdiction and liability to pursue war criminals discovered living under new identities in the United States. In 2017, for example, notorious Liberian warlord Mohammed Jabbateh was prosecuted after he was discovered residing in East Lansdowne, Pennsylvania. Prosecutors relied on Jabbateh's violation of U.S. immigration law to establish jurisdiction, and then brought forward seventeen Liberian witnesses who testified that Jabbateh had murdered and maimed civilians, sexually enslaved women, conscripted child soldiers, desecrated corpses, and committed cannibalism. Jabbateh was convicted and sentenced to 30 years in prison — for having lied about his past in immigration documents. U.S. Immigration & Customs Enforcement, *Liberian Warlord "Jungle Jabbah" Receives Historic Sentence in Immigration Fraud Case,* Apr. 20, 2018, https://www.ice.gov/news/releases/liberian-warlord-jungle-jabbah-receives-historic-sentence-immigration-fraud-case.

If foreign cases indeed evolve into a customary international law norm, might universal jurisdiction also be invoked in U.S. courts to enforce IHL and prosecute war crimes where statutory gaps otherwise prevent prosecution?

———————————

[NSL p. 343. Insert at the end of the first full paragraph.]

S.J. Res. 12 was not enacted into law. But in February 2020, the Trump administration entered into an agreement with the Taliban in Doha, Qatar to withdraw all U.S. troops from Afghanistan in return for a ceasefire and a political settlement between the Taliban and the Afghan government, and the Taliban's promise to prevent Al Qaeda and other terrorist groups from reestablishing bases there. Nevertheless, violence in the country has continued nearly unabated since that time. Taliban fighters have killed thousands of Afghan police and security forces, health workers, students, teachers, judges, and religious minorities, along with many civilians not specifically targeted. Among those killed were polio vaccinators and charity workers clearing land mines. They have also retaken control of roughly half of the country. The grisly toll is recounted in periodic reports from the *New York Times*. *See, e.g.*, Fatima Faizi & Najim Rahim, *Afghan War Casualty Report: June 2021*, N.Y. Times, June 17, 2021.

When President Trump declared in late 2020 that he would withdraw all U.S. military forces from Afghanistan, Congress specified in the William M. (Mac) Thornberry National Defense Authorization Act for Fiscal Year 2021, Pub. L. No. 116-283, §1215, 134 Stat. 3388, 3921-3922 (2021), that no funds should be expended to reduce the number of troops deployed there below a certain number unless the President submitted either an extensive report on U.S. military operations in Afghanistan or a waiver explaining how a drawdown was "important to the national security interests of the United States." *Id.* §1215(b), (d). But at the end of the Trump administration, the report/waiver requirement apparently was ignored, and by mid-January 2021, all but 2,500 U.S. troops had been withdrawn. Idrees Ali, *U.S. Troops in Afghanistan Now Down to 2,500, Lowest since 2001: Pentagon*, Reuters, Jan. 15, 2021.

In April 2021, President Biden announced the withdrawal of all remaining U.S. forces, White House, *Remarks by President Biden on the Way Forward in Afghanistan*, Apr. 14, 2021, and both U.S. and NATO troops were set to leave Afghanistan by the end of August 2021. Questions remain, however, about the nature and extent of ongoing support for Afghan government forces. *See* Clayton Thomas, *Afghanistan: Background and U.S. Policy: In Brief* (Cong. Res. Serv. R45122), June 11, 2021.

[NSL p. 364. Insert at the end of Note 4.]

In December 2018, President Trump announced the full withdrawal of some 2,000-2,500 U.S. military forces still in Syria, prompting the resignation of Defense Secretary James Mattis. *See* Mark Landler, Helene Cooper & Eric Schmitt, *Trump Withdraws U.S. Forces From Syria, Declaring "We Have Won Against ISIS"*, N.Y. Times, Dec. 19, 2018; Helene Cooper, *Jim Mattis, Defense Secretary, Resigns in Rebuke of Trump's Worldview*, N.Y. Times, Dec. 20, 2018. Two months later, the White House declared that about 200 troops would remain as a "peacekeeping force." Alex Johnson, *U.S. to Leave about 200 Troops in Syria, White House Says*, NBC News, Feb. 21, 2019. Nevertheless, an estimated 800 remained there a year later. Miriam Berger, *Where U.S. Troops Are in the Middle East and Afghanistan, Visualized*, Wash. Post, Jan. 4, 2020. In September 2020, the Pentagon sent another 100 troops, armored vehicles, and other equipment to Syria to counter Russian activities, on the same day that Trump declared that U.S. forces "are out of Syria" except to guard oil fields in the region. Eric Schmitt, *U.S. Sending More Troops to Syria to Counter the Russians*, N.Y. Times, Sept. 18, 2020.

In November 2020, the State Department's Special Representative for Syria Engagement, James F. Jeffrey, revealed that the number of U.S. troops remaining in Syria was "a lot more than" the 200 authorized by President Trump. "We were always playing shell games to not make clear to our leadership how many troops we had there," he said. Katie Bo Williams, *Outgoing Syria Envoy Admits Hiding US Troop Numbers*, Defense One, Nov. 12, 2020. Presumably, however, the Defense Department always knew how many of its personnel were deployed in the country.

What does this record suggest about the Commander in Chief's ability to execute U.S. foreign policy or to direct the use of its armed forces? About the ability of Congress and the American public to monitor U.S. military activities abroad and to hold government officials accountable for those activities?

In February 2021, President Biden ordered air strikes against targets in Syria in response to rocket attacks by Iranian-backed militias on U.S. forces in Iraq. In a report to Congress under the War Powers Resolution, he said he acted "consistent with my responsibility to protect United States citizens both at home and abroad and in furtherance of United States national security and foreign policy interests, pursuant to my constitutional authority to conduct United States foreign relations and as Commander in Chief and Chief Executive." But he did not invoke either the 2001 AUMF or the 2002 Iraq War resolution. The White House, Letter to the Speaker of the House and President Pro Tempore of the Senate Consistent with the War Powers Resolution (Feb. 27, 2021). The report also claimed that "[t]he United States took this action pursuant to the United States' inherent right of self-defense as reflected in Article 51 of the United Nations Charter." And it declared U.S. readiness to use force when "the government of [a] state . . . is unwilling or unable to prevent the use of its territory by non-state militia groups" to attack "our personnel and our partners." Can you briefly cite authorities for each of these claims? *See* Rebecca Ingber, *Legally Sliding into War*, Just Security, Mar. 15, 2021 (expressing doubt about such claims).

In May 2021, nearly 1,000 U.S. troops reportedly remained in eastern Syria to fight remnants of ISIS forces and prevent them from regrouping. Lolita C. Baldor, *US Central Command Chief: Important to Keep Pressure on ISIS*, AP, May 23, 2021.

[NSL p. 367. Insert before 2. Iran.]

In July 2020, members of both parties introduced a far more modest proposal:

H.R. 7500
116th Cong., 2d Sess.
July 9, 2020

Sec. 1. Short title.

This Act may be cited as the "Limit on the Expansion of the Authorization for Use of Military Force Act".

Sec. 2. Limitation on expansion of the 2001 authorization for use of military force.

The Authorization for Use of Military Force (Public Law 107-40; 50 U.S.C. 1541 note) may not be construed to provide authorization for the use of force, including under section 5(b) of the War Powers Resolution (50 U.S.C. 1544(b)), in any country in which United States Armed Forces are not engaged in hostilities pursuant to such Authorization as of the date of the enactment of this Act.

Sec. 3. Rule of construction.

Nothing in this Act may be construed —
(1) to deem the use of force in any country in which United States Armed Forces are engaged in hostilities as of the date of the enactment of this Act as lawful or unlawful pursuant to the Authorization for Use of Military Force (Public Law 107-40; 50 U.S.C. 1541 note); or
(2) as an authorization for use of military force.

According to the sponsors of H.R. 7500, "In the event that the president must act to defend the United States in a country where we are not operating today, he could do so under the terms laid out in the War Powers Resolution of 1973." Anthony Brown et al., Opinion, *Bipartisan Lawmakers Introduce Bill to Limit Further Expansion of 2001 Authorization for Use of Military Force*, The Hill, July 9, 2020. Can you describe the circumstances under which this statement might be true?

Did this measure answer the objections raised by President Trump a year earlier? Can you guess why the bill never made it out of committee?

[NSL p. 369. Insert at the end of Note 1.]

Neither of the 2019 bills was enacted into law. In 2020, following the United States' targeted killing of Maj. Gen. Qassim Soleimani, head of Iran's Quds Force, both the Senate and House passed a resolution that declared,

> The conflict between the United States and the Islamic Republic of Iran constitutes, within the meaning of section 4(a) of the War Powers Resolution (50 U.S.C. 1543(a)), either hostilities or a situation where imminent involvement in hostilities is clearly indicated by the circumstances into which United States Armed Forces have been introduced. [S.J. Res. 68, 116th Cong. §1(4) (2020).]

The resolution went on to direct the President to "terminate the use of United States Armed Forces against the Islamic Republic of Iran . . . unless explicitly authorized by a declaration of war or specific authorization for use of military force against Iran." *Id.* §2(a). The 2020 bill was approved by both houses, but failed when the Senate was unable to override President Trump's veto.

If S.J. Res. 68 had been enacted, would it have been constitutional? Do you think a court would have ordered the withdrawal of U.S. troops confronting Iranian forces in the Middle East under §5(b) of the War Powers Resolution (casebook p. 91)? Would any court have ordered the President to halt an attack on Iran, either one that was planned or one that was already underway? Who, if anyone, would have had standing to maintain a suit to order compliance with the legislation?

[NSL p. 397, CTL p. 157. Replace the second paragraph of Note 6 with the following.]

In October 2017 President Trump replaced the 2013 Obama administration *U.S. Policy Standards* with a more flexible regimen. It permitted commanders in the field to decide whether to target suspects based on their status as members of a terrorist group, rather than on their conduct, as long as conditions specified in the new general operating principles for that area had been met. The "operating principles" stated that there should be "near certainty" that civilians "will not be injured or killed in the course of operations," but that "variations" could be made "where necessary" so long as commanders followed certain procedures.

The Trump administration did not make its new framework for drone strikes public. The rules for "direct action" operations — including drone strikes and commando raids outside conventional war zones — were disclosed by the Biden administration with some redactions in 2021 in response to Freedom of Information Act lawsuits brought by the *New York Times* and the American Civil Liberties Union. Charlie Savage, *Trump's Secret Rules for Drone Strikes Outside War Zones Are Disclosed*, N.Y. Times, May 1, 2021. The redacted eleven-page Trump administration *Principles, Standards, and Procedures for U.S. Direct Action Against Terrorist Targets* (n.d.) is available here: https://int.nyt.com/data/documenttools/trump-psp-drone-strike-rules-foia/52f4a4baf5fc54c5/full.pdf. For analysis of the Trump rules and a critique of U.S. targeting policies and practices as threats to cornerstone principles of international law, see Hina Shamsi, *Trump's Secret Rules for Drone Strikes and Presidents' Unchecked License to Kill*, Just Security, May 3, 2021.

The Biden administration suspended the Trump rules on January 20, 2021, and replaced them with an interim policy that requires White House approval for strikes outside of active war zones in Afghanistan, Iraq, and Syria. Administration officials then began a review toward developing a new policy. Savage, *supra*. The policy had not been announced as of June 2021.

Does suspension of the Trump administration drone strike policies and a requirement for White House sign-off on targeting outside conventional war zones align U.S. practices with IHL and HRL? If not, what reforms should a new administration policy include to bring them into compliance with international law?

If the Biden administration completes its withdrawal of forces from Afghanistan (now set for September 2021), what targeting rules will govern a proposed drone strike directed at a suspected Taliban fighter who is believed to be planning an imminent attack on civilians in Kabul?

[NSL p. 409, CTL p. 169. Insert at the end of Note 5.]

The D.C. Circuit affirmed dismissal in *Kareem v. Haspel,* 986 F.3d 859 (D.C. Cir. 2021). But instead of finding the lawsuit barred by the state secrets privilege, the unanimous panel found that journalist Kareem's allegations did not create a plausible inference that the United States government had designated him as a terrorist target for lethal force, and therefore that he lacked Article III standing to challenge the alleged designation.

[NSL p. 411, CTL p. 171. Add the following Section.]

E. CASE STUDY: TARGETING GENERAL SOLEIMANI

In the early hours of January 3, 2020, U.S. forces launched a drone strike that killed General Qassem Soleimani, head of the Islamic Revolutionary Guard Corps-Quds Force (IRGC-QF) of Iran, as he departed the Baghdad airport. Iran has been designated by the United States as a state sponsor of terrorism, and the IRGC-QF is its expeditionary terrorist force, which has itself been designated by the United States as a Specially Designated Global Terrorist and a Foreign Terrorist Organization. The IRGC-QF "spearheaded a closely coordinated campaign to equip the [Iraqi] Shi'a militia for proxy warfare," targeting U.S. service members, among others. *Karcher v. Islamic Rep. of Iran*, 396 F. Supp. 3d 12, 22-25 (D.D.C. 2019) (describing attacks on U.S. personnel in great detail). The campaign killed at least 603 U.S. soldiers and severely injured many others. *See* Kyle Rempfer, *Iran Killed More US Troops in Iraq than Previously Known, Pentagon Says*, Military Times, Apr. 4, 2019.

Consider the targeted killing of Soleimani in light of the international and domestic legal regimes that arguably apply — human rights law, IHL, the executive order ban on assassination, and other domestic law.

Human Rights Law. Soleimani was not directly engaged in unlawful violence at the time of the strike (he was reportedly driving to meet the Iraqi Prime Minister). But he was notorious for directing terrorist attacks in Iraq at civilians, government officials, and Coalition Forces since at least 2006. A Defense Department spokesperson asserted that

> In the weeks preceding the air strike against Soleimani, provocations against the United States intensified with a series of attacks by Iran-supported militias on U.S. personnel and property in Iraq. KH, the Qods Force-backed Shia militia group, fired rockets at bases in Iraq where U.S. forces are located. Between November 9 and December 9, 2019, Qods Force-backed militia groups fired rockets at the Qayyarah West Air Base, Al Asad Air Base, and the Baghdad Embassy complex. Then, on December 27, KH attacked the K-1 Air Base in Kirkuk, killing a U.S. contractor and injuring U.S. and Iraqi military personnel. In response, U.S. forces struck a number of KH installations in Iraq and Syria to degrade the group's ability to launch additional attacks. Then, on December 31, KH and other Iran-backed militia groups organized a demonstration that turned violent at the U.S. Embassy in Baghdad, inflicting significant damage to U.S. property and imperiling U.S. lives. [Paul C. Ney, General Counsel, U.S. Dep't of Defense, *Legal Considerations Related to the U.S. Air Strike Against Qassem Soleimani* (Mar. 4, 2020), https://assets.documentcloud.org/documents/6808252/DOD-GC-Speech-BYU-QS.pdf]

Did the Soleimani operation violate human rights law? Should that law's "imminence" requirement be given a more elastic construction to include a history of terrorist attacks that attests to both the ability and the intent of the target to attack again?

IHL. How does the targeted killing of Soleimani fare in light of the debates about status and conduct-based targeting? Consider the Defense Department's justification for Soleimani's killing:

> Attacks against U.S. forces and interests were assessed to be highly likely to continue in the absence of a military response in self-defense to restore deterrence.
>
> Moreover, the strike on January 2d was also consistent with the international law requirement that our measures in self-defense be "proportionate to the nature of the threat being addressed." As DoD communicated to the public at the time, "General Soleimani was actively developing plans to attack American diplomats and service members in Iraq and throughout the region." "He had orchestrated attacks on coalition bases in Iraq over the last several months," and he also approved the demonstration that turned violent at the U.S. Embassy in Baghdad just two days earlier on December 31. Targeting the Iranian commander responsible for orchestrating, planning, and

supporting recent attacks against the United States and planning new attacks was a proportionate response to the threat of such attacks.

Some have questioned whether another Iranian armed attack against the United States was "imminent" at the time of the strike targeting Soleimani. This is a red herring, as the saying goes. Under international law, an imminent attack is not a necessary condition for resort to force in self-defense in this circumstance because armed attacks by Iran already had occurred and were expected to occur again. Of course, although such analysis was not necessary in this case given this recent history of past attacks, the threat of an imminent armed attack can also justify a resort to force under international law. [Ney, *supra*.]

Did General Counsel Ney correctly apply international law to the Soleimani targeting?

Applying U.S. Law. Did the Executive Order 12,333 ban on assassination apply to the killing of Soleimani? On the one hand, he was certainly a "high-level belligerent leader" arguably killed in national self-defense against the terrorist attacks the IRGC-QF orchestrated. On the other hand, he was arguably targeted "for political reasons," as the foreign official commanding the IRGC-QF — to send a signal to Iran.

Did President Trump's approval of the strike operate as a waiver of the executive order ban? In light of the suspension of the Trump rules by President Biden, would the Biden administration have approved the Soleimani strike in 2021? On what legal bases?

[NSL p. 415. Insert at the end of the second paragraph after the boxed text.]

Speaking days after ransomware attacks on U.S. energy and private infrastructure sectors, Energy Secretary Jennifer Granholm was asked whether the nation's adversaries have the capability of shutting down the power grid. Granholm said, "Yeah, they do." Chandelis Duster, *Energy Secretary Says Adversaries Have Capability of Shutting Down U.S. Power Grid*, CNN, June 6, 2021.

[NSL p. 416. Insert before Part B.]

In early 2020, hackers believed to be backed by the Russian government succeeded in stealing data from a number of U.S. government agencies, several foreign governments and international organizations, and thousands of non-government entities. The operation was called SolarWinds, for one of the makers of software breached in the attack. One year later, Chinese government hackers launched an operation known as Microsoft Exchange, which reportedly breached tens of thousands of organizations in the United States and around the world. Experts warned that these exfiltration intrusions may have created back doors that could enable future attacks on physical infrastructure.

In May 2021, a ransomware attack prompted closing of the Colonial Pipeline, which carries refined gasoline and jet fuel from Texas up the East Coast to New York. Attackers penetrated the corporate owner's computer networks and held data hostage until they were paid a ransom demand. The pipeline operator, fearing that the hackers had obtained information that would enable them to attack pumping stations and controls, shut down 5,500 miles of pipeline carrying 45 percent of the East Coast's fuel supplies. Other ransomware attacks have struck municipal police departments, hospitals treating coronavirus patients, and a range of manufacturers, many of which have tried to hide the attacks out of embarrassment that their systems were penetrated. The attackers have often used automated attack tools and demanded ransom payments in cryptocurrencies, making them harder to trace. *See* David E. Sanger, Clifford Krauss & Nicole Perlroth, *Cyberattack Forces a Shutdown of a Top U.S. Pipeline*, N.Y. Times, May 8, 2021; Ellen Nakashima & Rachel Lerman, *Ransomware Is a National Security Threat and a Big Business — and It's Wreaking Havoc*, Wash. Post, May 15, 2021.

[NSL p. 419. Insert after the first paragraph of Note 1.]

At the 31st summit of NATO in Brussels in June 2021, the leaders of the 30 NATO countries agreed that "the impact of significant malicious cumulative cyber activities might, in certain circumstances, be considered as amounting to an armed attack," which could lead to invocation of Article 5 of the NATO treaty, triggering a commitment to mutual self-defense. See casebook pp. 341-342. Such decisions would be taken by the North Atlantic Council "on a case-by-case basis." Jennifer Hansler, *NATO Agrees Cyberattacks Could Amount to Armed Attacks and Lead to Invocation of Mutual Self-Defense Clause*, CNN, June 14, 2021. What is the legal significance of the NATO pledge?

[NSL p. 428. Insert after the DOD Cyber Strategy.]

On May 12, 2021, President Biden signed Executive Order No. 14,028, *Improving the Nation's Cybersecurity*, 86 Fed. Reg. 26633. Prompted at least in part by vulnerabilities exposed by the SolarWinds and Microsoft Exchange hacks noted *supra*, the order requires private firms that supply IT/OT services or products to federal agencies to promptly report cyber threats and incidents, and to cooperate in addressing those incidents. It also directs improved Internet cloud security inside the federal government, and software supply chain security, applying criteria set by the National Institute of Standards and Technology (NIST).

The order creates a Cyber Safety Review Board, an interagency group convened by DHS that includes private sector appointees, to review significant cyber incidents and to disseminate lessons learned. The order additionally requires the Cybersecurity and Infrastructure Security Agency (CISA), part of DHS, to develop a standardized incident response playbook for all federal agencies, while it weeds out and replaces inconsistent or outdated response plans. A parallel provision in the FY2021 NDAA authorizes CISA "with or without advance notice to or authorization from agencies" to hunt for and identify threats and vulnerabilities within federal systems. William M. (Mac) Thornberry National Defense Authorization Act for Fiscal Year 2021, Pub. L. No. 116-283, §1705, 134 Stat. 3388, 4082 (2021). Finally, the executive order directs the Secretary of Defense to incorporate standards and guidelines set forth in the order for national security systems where applicable and appropriate.

The overarching objective of the order is software security. A variety of ransomware and critical infrastructure vulnerabilities are unaddressed by the order, however. For helpful analysis, see Robert Chesney & Trey Herr, *Everything You Need to Know About the New Executive Order on Cybersecurity*, Lawfare, May 13, 2021.

The FY2021 NDAA also established a new Office of the National Cyber Director. Pub. L. No. 116-283, §1752, 134 Stat. 4144-4149. The NCD is charged with leading interagency planning and operational coordination for cyber defense from a newly created National Cyber Defense Center. Suggestions for organizing and operating the new Center are offered in James N. Miller & Robert Butler, *Making the National Cyber Director Operational with a National Cyber Defense Center*, Lawfare, Mar. 24, 2021.

Finally, on March 3, 2021, President issued the *Interim National Security Strategic Guidance*, https://www.whitehouse.gov/wp-content/uploads/2021/03/NSC-1v2.pdf. Regarding cyber, the *Guidance* says this:

> We will renew our commitment to international engagement on cyber issues, working alongside our allies and partners to uphold existing and shape new global norms in cyberspace. And we will hold actors accountable for destructive, disruptive, or otherwise destabilizing malicious cyber activity, and respond swiftly and proportionately to cyberattacks by imposing substantial costs through cyber and noncyber means. [*Id.* at 18.]

[NSL p. 431. Add at the end of Note 3.]

For analysis of the domestic legal framework for military cyber operations, see Robert Chesney, *The Domestic Legal Framework for US Military Cyber Operations* (Hoover Institution Aegis Series Paper No. 2003, July 29, 2020), https://s3.documentcloud.org/documents/7014455/Chesney-Webreadypdf.pdf.

[NSL p. 432. Add after Note 5.]

6. Weapons of Mass Destruction? The SolarWinds and Microsoft Exchange Hacks. In December 2020, the cyber security firm FireEye learned that an estimated 250 companies and federal agencies had been hit with one of the biggest cyberattacks in history. Hackers believed to be agents of the Russian foreign intelligence service, SVR, embedded malware into a software upgrade from SolarWinds, a Texas-based IT company, in an operation spanning at least nine months. When customers downloaded the upgrade, the malware exposed their systems to the hackers, who then used multiple strategies to compromise the networks of private firms, including Microsoft, and government agencies, including the Pentagon, State Department, and Department of Justice.

Not one of the threat detection mechanisms installed in government or private sector IT systems was tripped by the hacks. Notably, the hackers launched their attacks from inside the United States, avoiding surveillance that might have detected them if they had come from abroad.

Meanwhile, in March 2021 cybersecurity researchers discovered that state-sponsored Chinese hackers used a defect in Microsoft's Exchange server software to gain access to the e-mail servers of about 30,000

American businesses and organizations. These hackers installed malware that will allow them to return to the same IT systems in the future.

Since an anonymous group calling itself the Shadow Brokers stole and then released a cache of NSA hacking tools in 2017, and WikiLeaks organized and archived Vault 7, additional hacking tools developed by or for the CIA, hackers all over the world have been able infiltrate government and private sector networks on a massive scale. This virtual smorgasbord of hacking tools can give intruders access to critical infrastructure, including nuclear facilities, the electric grid, industrial control systems, air traffic control, and waterworks. In malicious hands, these tools can become weapons of mass destruction. They may be wielded by adversary nations, such as Russia or China, or by criminal or terrorist groups.

Much of the reporting on SolarWinds and similar threats has been led by Nicole Perlroth for the *New York Times*, who published *This Is How They Tell Me the World Ends: The Cyberweapons Arms Race* (2021). *See also* Herb Lin, *Reflections on the SolarWinds Breach*, Lawfare, Dec. 22, 2020; Joe Weiss & Bob Hunter, *The SolarWinds Hack Can Directly Affect Control Systems*, Lawfare, Jan. 22, 2021.

The United States has responded to the Russian cyber threat tit-for-tat — penetrating Russian systems with malware enabling access to critical infrastructure in that country. Are such responses lawful? What other lawful steps might the United States take to improve its cyber defenses?

[NSL p. 440. Add after third full paragraph.]

In 2020, the Pentagon declared that

> [d]espite concerted US efforts to reduce the role of nuclear weapons in international affairs and to negotiate reductions in the number of nuclear weapons, since 2010 no potential adversary has reduced either the role of nuclear weapons in its national security strategy or the number of nuclear weapons it fields. Rather, they have moved decidedly in the opposite direction. As a result, there is an increased potential for regional conflicts involving nuclear-armed adversaries in several parts of the world and the potential for adversary nuclear escalation in crisis or conflict. [Dep't of Defense, Jt. Pub. 3-72, *Joint Nuclear Operations* 1-1 (Apr. 17, 2020).]

See also Pentagon Sees "Increased Potential" for Nuclear Conflict, Secrecy News, July 6, 2021. In 2021, the *Bulletin of the Atomic Scientists* moved the hands of its Doomsday Clock to just 100 seconds before midnight (a nuclear apocalypse), the closest those hands have been in 75 years. Science & Security Bd., Bull. of Atomic Scientists, *It Is 100 Seconds to Midnight*, Bull. of Atomic Scientists, Jan. 27, 2021.

[NSL p. 444. Insert at the end of the first full paragraph.]

Near the end of his administration, President Trump reportedly sought to renegotiate New START, but he refused to extend it without conditions for an additional five-year term. *See* Paul Sonne, *Threat from Nuclear Weapons and Missiles Has Grown since Trump Entered Office*, Wash. Post, Oct. 12, 2020. Newly elected President Biden and Russian President Putin then agreed to extend the treaty for another five years. Vladimir Isachenkov, *Russia, US Exchange Documents to Extend Nuclear Pact*, AP, Jan. 26, 2021.

[NSL p. 445. Insert at the end of the second full paragraph.]

In November 2020, despite expressions of regret from European allies, the Trump administration formally withdrew from the Open Skies Treaty, claiming violations by Russia. Ryan Browne, *US Formally Withdraws from Open Skies Treaty That Bolstered European Security*, CNN, Nov. 22, 2020. Its withdrawal ended periodic Russian overflights of U.S. territory, and left the United States to rely on satellite imagery to monitor military activities in Russia. Shortly thereafter, Russia announced that it, too, would withdraw from the treaty. Anton Troianovski & David E. Sanger, *Russia's Exit from Open Skies Treaty May Complicate Relations with Biden Team*, N.Y. Times, Jan. 16, 2021.

[NSL p. 455. Insert before Notes and Questions.]

By mid-2021, 86 states (none possessing nuclear weapons) had signed the treaty, and 54 had ratified or acceded to it, bringing the treaty into force.

[NSL p. 458. Insert after the first full paragraph.]

Questions about sole presidential control of nuclear weapons were raised again 46 years later, when President Donald J. Trump underwent treatment for the COVID-19 virus. One of the drugs administered to him for several days, dexamethasone, is said by doctors to make some patients paranoid and delusional, and to create feelings of euphoria and invulnerability. But despite these concerns, Trump declined to invoke the 25th Amendment and turn over control temporarily to the Vice President. David E. Sanger & William J. Broad, *Trump's Health Revives Questions About Unchecked Nuclear Authority*, N.Y. Times, Oct. 12, 2020.

[NSL p. 464. Insert at the end of Note 5.]

When President Donald Trump appeared to encourage an attack by his supporters on the U.S. Capitol on January 6, 2021, new questions arose about his mental state and fitness for office. Some recalled similar concerns in 1974 about President Nixon, who, like Trump, faced the prospect of impeachment.

House Speaker Nancy Pelosi, calling the President "unhinged," asked the Chairman of the Joint Chiefs of Staff, General Mark Milley, about "available precautions for preventing an unstable president from initiating military hostilities and ordering a nuclear strike." David E. Sanger & Eric Schmitt, *Pelosi Pressed Pentagon on Safeguards to Prevent Trump from Initiating Strikes*, N.Y. Times, Jan. 9, 2021. Chairman Milley's precise response was not reported. But some DOD officials noted that so long as the President remained in office, his legal orders as Commander in Chief would be followed. Removal of the President from the chain of command would constitute a military coup, they said. How would you have answered Speaker Pelosi's inquiry?

[NSL p. 492, CTL p. 178. Insert before The Idealized Intelligence Cycle graphic.]

The National Intelligence Priorities Framework (NIPF) has become the single most important administrative tool for managing the overall U.S. intelligence apparatus. The NIPF is used to determine priorities for collection and to allocate resources based on them. In January 2021, outgoing Director of National Intelligence John Ratcliffe issued Intelligence Community Directive 204, *National Intelligence Priorities Framework* (Jan. 7, 2021), https://fas.org/irp/dni/icd/icd-204.pdf, which defines policy "for setting national intelligence priorities, translating them into action, and evaluating Intelligence Community (IC) responsiveness to them." *Id.* The 2021 directive replaces a 2015 NIPF issued by President Obama.

[NSL p. 513, CTL p. 199. Replace the first full paragraph on the page with the following.]

Every president since Truman has personalized the organization of the NSC and its staff and functions. President Biden signed *National Security Memorandum 2 (NSM-2), Memorandum on Renewing the National Security Council System* (Feb. 4, 2021), https://www.whitehouse.gov/briefing-room/statements-releases/2021/02/04/memorandum-renewing-the-national-security-council-system/. In addition to the statutory members of the NSC specified in the National Security Act, additional members include the Attorney General, the Secretary of Homeland Security, the National Security Adviser, and the President's Chief of Staff. President Biden's NSC also includes the Ambassador to the United Nations, the Director of the Office of Science and Technology Policy (OSTP), and the Administrator of the U.S. Agency for International Development (USAID). The CIA Director will be an additional adviser. The memorandum lists other officials who may be included "as appropriate" or "depending on the issue," including the EPA Administrator, Secretary of Labor, Secretary of Health and Human Services, the National Cyber Director (a new position created by the FY2021 National Defense Authorization Act), the Deputy National Security Adviser for Cybersecurity, the COVID-19 Response Coordinator, and the Special Presidential Envoy for Climate. *See id.*

[NSL p. 563. Insert after Note 7.]

8. Covert Action and Cyber Operations. As declared in the Defense Department's *Cyber Strategy 2018* and reinforced with statutory authority in the FY2019 National Defense Authorization Act (casebook pp. 428-431), the United States promises to "defend forward to disrupt or halt malicious cyber activity at its source, including activity that falls below the level of armed conflict." *Cyber Strategy* at 1. In July 2020, a news report indicated that around the time of issuance of the new strategy and enactment of new statutory cyber authority, President Trump signed a sweeping intelligence finding granting the CIA express authorization to conduct its own cyber operations without requiring further White House or National Security Council approval. Like the *Cyber Strategy* and FY2019 NDAA, the finding reportedly authorized offensive cyber operations directed at "a handful of adversarial countries," including Russia, China, and North Korea. Zach Dorfman et al., *Exclusive: Secret Trump Order Gives CIA More Powers to Launch Cyberattacks*, Yahoo News, July 15, 2020, https://www.yahoo.com/now/secret-trump-order-gives-cia-more-powers-to-launch-cyberattacks-090015219.html. Since the finding was signed in 2018, according to the report, the CIA has carried out at least a dozen cyber operations. *Id.*

How will the CIA operations avoid conflict with Defense Department "defending forward" cyber operations? How will Congress conduct oversight of the CIA operations if the finding identifies neither an enemy nor a set of objectives? For analysis of these and related questions, see Robert Chesney, *The CIA, Covert Action and Operations in Cyberspace*, Lawfare, July 15, 2020.

[NSL p. 580, CTL p. 232. After the first paragraph replace the second bullet with this one.]

- routine searches for public health purposes. *Camara v. Municipal Court*, 387 U.S. 523 (1967); *See v. City of Seattle*, 387 U.S. 541 (1967).

[NSL p. 598, CTL p. 250. Add after the last full paragraph.]

In the years since *Jones*, GPS and other location services on our devices have become even more widespread. In *Carpenter v. United States*, 138 S. Ct. 2206 (2018), the Supreme Court held that the Constitution requires the government to obtain a warrant to compel cell phone companies to turn over location data about their customers. (*Carpenter* is separately considered NSL pp. 685, 722; CTL pp. 337, 374.)

What if the government is able to buy similar location data from a private broker? Is a warrant required? Apparently, the government does not think so. For example, the Defense Intelligence Agency (DIA) asserted in a memorandum its belief that "the Carpenter decision [does not] require a judicial warrant endorsing purchase or use of commercially available data for intelligence purposes." Charlie Savage, *Intelligence Analysts Use U.S. Smartphone Location Data Without Warrants, Memo Says*, N.Y. Times, Jan. 22, 2021. Although DIA apparently buys location data for investigations about foreign persons abroad, the broker it buys from does not separate American and foreign users. The Department of Homeland Security reportedly reached a similar conclusion that its personnel could purchase location data for law enforcement by Immigration and Customs Enforcement and Customs and Border Protection. *Id.* The IRS also asserted authority to purchase location data without a warrant, but the Treasury Department's Inspector General expressed skepticism that government acquisition of such data is consistent with *Carpenter. See* Chris Mills Rodrigo, *Watchdog Questions Legality of Using Cellphone Data Without Warrants*, The Hill, Feb. 22, 2021.

[NSL p. 624, CTL p. 276. Insert after the third full paragraph.]

The lone wolf provision has been subject to sunset and then renewed more than once since 2004. When the most recent sunset loomed in late 2019, a short-term extension continued the lone wolf authority until March 2020. In the midst of heavily politicized debates over FISA and its reform, Congress then failed to renew it. *See* Margaret Taylor, *The Specter of FISA Reform Haunts Capitol Hill*, Lawfare, May 29, 2020. It is therefore no longer in force as of this writing.

[NSL p. 625, CTL p. 277. Insert after the first paragraph of Note 2.]

A review of the initial Carter Page FISA application as well as three subsequent applications for renewal by the Department of Justice's Office of the Inspector General (OIG) found no evidence of politically motivated investigative activity, but it did find significant errors or omissions in the initial application, including factual misstatements that "made it appear that the information supporting probable cause was stronger than was actually the case." Off. of the Inspector Gen'l, U.S. Dep't of Justice, *Review of Four FISA Applications and Other Aspects of the FBI's Crossfire Hurricane Investigation* 16 (Dec. 2019), https://www.justice.gov/storage/120919-examination.pdf. As the FISA Court summarized, the claim was that "personnel of the Federal Bureau of Investigation (FBI) provided false information to the National Security Division (NSD) of the Department of Justice, and withheld material information from NSD which was detrimental to the FBI's case . . . ." *In re Accuracy Concerns Regarding FBI Matters Submitted to the FISC*, 411 F. Supp. 3d 333, 334 (FISA Ct. 2019). Such inaccuracies are particularly problematic given the unique nature of the FISC's operations. Because the proceedings are ex parte, "the FISC relies on the U.S. government's 'full and accurate presentation of the facts to make its probable cause determinations'" and on the case agents "to ensure that statements contained in applications submitted to the FISC are 'scrupulously accurate.'" Off. of the Inspector Gen'l, *supra*, at 43.

Following issuance of the OIG report, the government advised the FISC that it was sequestering collection associated with Foreign Intelligence Surveillance Act applications targeting Carter W. Page based upon its determination that at least the third and fourth FISA applications targeting Page lacked sufficient predication to establish probable cause that Page was acting as an agent of a foreign power.

The numerous flaws in the Page applications prompted the DOJ IG to dig deeper into the FBI's FISA application practices to determine whether these problems represented an anomaly. They did not. A subsequent review of 29 FISA applications found discrepancies and errors in each of them that led the OIG to declare that it had "no confidence" in the effectiveness of the FBI's internal procedures designed to ensure the accuracy of applications. *See* Off. of the Inspector Gen'l, *Management Advisory Memorandum for the Director of the Federal Bureau of Investigation Regarding the Execution of Woods Procedures for Applications Filed with the Foreign Intelligence Surveillance Court Relating to U.S. Persons* 7-8 (Mar. 2020). In the wake of this report the FISA Court ordered the government to conduct its own internal audit into these 29 applications. That audit characterized most of the errors the IG had identified as nonmaterial, and expressed the view that neither the one material misstatement nor the one material omission the government found would have invalidated the underlying FISC order. *See In re Accuracy Concerns Regarding FBI Matters Submitted to the FISC* (FISA Ct. July 29, 2020), https://assets.documentcloud.org/documents/7013140/NSD-Review-of-Woods-ProceduresIGAudit.pdf.

Although FBI Acting General Counsel Dawn Browning stated that the review "should instill confidence in the FBI's use of its FISA authorities," Jeremy Gordon, *Justice Department Completes Reviews of Errors in FISA Applications*, Lawfare, Aug. 11, 2020, the two reports fueled reform proposals, some internal to the Justice Department and FBI, others in the form of proposed statutory revisions to the basic FISA process. The DOJ IG as well as an amicus appointed by the FISC to consider necessary reforms suggested a host of changes to address these findings. Measures immediately adopted by the FBI Director included new standards and procedures to "enhance accuracy and completeness" of FISA applications, enhanced training, and more robust audits and reviews "to ensure [these reforms] to the FISA process are effective." Letter Brief of David Kris, Amicus Curiae, *In re Accuracy Concerns Regarding FBI Matters Submitted to the FISC Docket*, No. Misc. 19-02 (FISA Ct. Jan. 15, 2020), *available at* https://www.fisc.uscourts.gov/ sites/default/files/FISC%20Misc%2019%2002%20Amicus%20Curiae% 20letter%20brief%20January%2015%202020%20200115.pdf.

Bills in Congress that would have added modest new protections to the FISA process generally were not enacted when, in March 2020, President Trump's tweeted veto threat effectively killed the prospects for reform. Benjamin Wittes, *The Ides of March Are Come: A Trump Tweet Causes FISA Authorities to Expire*, Lawfare, Mar. 16, 2020.

In a June 25, 2020 opinion, the FISC set parameters for the temporary retention, use, and disclosure of information acquired pursuant to the Page FISA applications with respect to: (1) ongoing Freedom of Information Act litigation with third-parties, (2) ongoing and potential civil litigation initiated by Mr. Page, (3) a review of FBI personnel's conduct in the Page investigation, (4) Department of Justice Office of Inspector General monitoring of the implementation of recommendations from its report, and (5) review of the conduct of government personnel in the Page investigation and the broader "Crossfire Hurricane" investigation of Russian interference in the 2016 Presidential election. The government did not seek, nor did the FISC authorize, the retention, use, or disclosure of the relevant FISA information for intelligence purposes. *See In re Page*, No. 16-1182 (FISA Ct. June 25, 2020), https://www.intelligence.gov/assets/documents/702%20Documents/ declassified/June_2020_FISC_Opinion.pdf.

Finally, the Privacy and Civil Liberties Oversight Board (PCLOB) obtained from the FBI and closely reviewed 19 FISA applications relating to counterterrorism investigations. The PCLOB's chairman issued a white paper that included additional recommendations for improving the FISA application process, particularly with respect to improving the efficiency of internal oversight procedures. *See* Adam Klein, *Chairman's White Paper: Oversight of the Foreign Intelligence Surveillance Act* (2021); Adam Klein, *What I Found in 19 FISA Applications*, Lawfare, June 18, 2021.

[NSL p. 627, CTL p. 279. Add at the end of Note 4.b.]

Like the lone wolf provision, roving wiretaps authority has been subject to repeated sunset and renewal. As another sunset loomed in late 2019, Congress approved a short-term extension, but then failed to reauthorize roving wiretaps. The authority also lapsed in March 2020.

See Margaret Taylor, *The Specter of FISA Reform Haunts Capitol Hill*, Lawfare, May 29, 2020.

[NSL p. 675, CTL p. 327. Insert at the end of Note 3.]

In December 2019, the FISC issued an 83-page ruling with a redacted case name approving new querying rules for Section 702 data. *[Redacted]* (FISA Ct. Dec. 6, 2019), https://www.intelligence.gov/assets/documents/702%20Documents/declassified/2019_702_Cert_FISC_O pinion_06Dec19_OCR.pdf. The heavily redacted opinion was released to the public on September 4, 2020, when it was declassified and published online by ODNI. Although presiding Judge James Boasberg approved the new rules for the FBI and NSA, he noted that "there still appear to be widespread violations of the querying standard by the FBI." *Id.* at 65. More specifically, many FBI queries failed to meet the querying standard requiring the queries to be "reasonably likely to retrieve foreign-intelligence information or evidence of a crime." *Id.* at 67. Judge Boasberg cited an example from August 2019, when the FBI made a query using the identifiers of about 16,000 people, even though only seven of them had ties to an investigation. *See id.* Moreover, on numerous occasions the FBI has employed U.S. person queries in circumstances requiring an order from the FISA Court without first acquiring such an order. Due to these ongoing compliance issues, Judge Boasberg announced that the FISA Court would continue to monitor the FBI's querying process closely. *See id.* at 79-83. In a similar vein, NSA chose to ignore a procedure designed to prevent the collection of domestic communications because they were concerned about losing foreign intelligence.

The ODNI also provided the targeting, minimization, and querying procedures for the FBI, NSA, CIA, and NCTC associated with the 2019 certifications. All of the documents are available in full-text searchable format at intel.gov (https://www.intel.gov/index.php/ic-on-the-record-database/results/995release-of-documents-related-to-the-2019-fisa-section-702-certifications) and IC on the Record (https://icontherecord.tumblr.com/post/628356110309572608/release-of-documents-related-to-the-2019fisa).

[NSL p. 677. CTL p. 329. Insert at the end of Note 9.]

In *United States v. Hasbajrami*, 945 F.3d 641 (2d Cir. 2019), the Second Circuit agreed with the Ninth Circuit in rejecting a Fourth

Amendment challenge to collecting intelligence on U.S. persons incident to lawful collection on a non-U.S. based foreign national abroad. However, the Second Circuit remanded the case to the district court because the record below did not show whether the government acted reasonably when it queried its databases for information linked to U.S. person Hasbajrami. Thus, according to the Second Circuit, regardless of Section 702 minimization procedures, querying is a separate Fourth Amendment event, and the district court is required to determine whether any search of Section 702-collected data violated the Fourth Amendment. *But see United States v. Muhtorov*, 187 F. Supp. 3d 1240, 1256 (D. Colo 2015) ("Accessing stored records in a database legitimately acquired is not a search in the context of the Fourth Amendment because there is no reasonable expectation of privacy in that information."); *[Redacted]*, Order at 33 (FISA Ct. Nov. 6, 2015) (rejecting argument from *amicus curiae* that U.S. person queries should be considered a "'separate Fourth Amendment event' that should be independently assessed").

[NSL p. 699, CTL p. 351. Insert at the end of Note 3.]

What if the government purchases location data from a private broker, instead of relying on a court order to require production of the information, as in *Carpenter*? Is a warrant required? Multiple federal agencies believe the answer is "no." The Defense Intelligence Agency, Customs and Border Protection, Immigration and Customs Enforcement, and the Internal Revenue Service all have asserted the right to purchase and access the contents of commercially available databases that include location data derived from smartphone apps without a warrant. *See* Charlie Savage, *Intelligence Analysts Use U.S. Smartphone Location Data Without Warrants, Memo Says*, N.Y. Times, Jan. 22, 2021; Chris Mills Rodrigo, *Watchdog Questions Legality of Using Cellphone Data Without Warrants*, The Hill, Feb. 22, 2021. In response to the IRS's claim of this authority, the Treasury Department's Inspector General expressed skepticism that government acquisition of such data is consistent with *Carpenter*. *See* Rodrigo, *supra*.

[NSL p. 707, CTL p. 359. Insert at the end of the second paragraph.]

In 2021, the business records provision reverted to the form it had in 1998, after more recent amendments expired pursuant to a sunset provision.

[NSL p. 727, CTL p. 379. Replace Note 6 with the following.]

6. Section 215 or Business Records Orders. As *Doe I* notes, agencies and grand juries have long used subpoenas to collect third-party records. A 1998 amendment to FISA gave the FISC equivalent authority to issue production orders for certain business records on application by the FBI:

Intelligence Authorization Act for 1999
Pub. L. No. 105-272, 112 Stat. 2396, 2411-2412 (1998)

Sec. 501. Definitions

As used in this title:

(1) The terms "foreign power", "agent of a foreign power", "foreign intelligence information", "international terrorism", and "Attorney General" shall have the same meanings as in section 101 of this Act.

(2) The term "common carrier" means any person or entity transporting people or property by land, rail, water, or air for compensation.

(3) The term "physical storage facility" means any business or entity that provides space for the storage of goods or materials, or services related to the storage of goods or materials, to the public or any segment thereof.

(4) The term "public accommodation facility" means any inn, hotel, motel, or other establishment that provides lodging to transient guests.

(5) The term "vehicle rental facility" means any person or entity that provides vehicles for rent, lease, loan, or other similar use to the public or any segment thereof.

Sec. 502. Access to Certain Business Records for Foreign Intelligence and International Terrorism Investigations

(a) The Director of the Federal Bureau of Investigation or a designee of the Director (whose rank shall be no lower than Assistant Special Agent in Charge) may make an application for an order authorizing a common carrier, public accommodation facility, physical storage facility, or vehicle rental facility to release records in its possession for an investigation to gather foreign intelligence information or an investigation concerning international terrorism

> which investigation is being conducted by the Federal Bureau of
> Investigation under such guidelines as the Attorney General approves
> pursuant to Executive Order No. 12333, or a successor order.
>
>   (b) Each application under this section . . . .
>   (2) shall specify that —
>   (A) the records concerned are sought for an investigation
>   described in subsection (a); and
>   (B) there are specific and articulable facts giving reason
>   to believe that the person to whom the records pertain is a
>   foreign power or an agent of a foreign power. . . .
>   (d) . . .
>   (2) No common carrier, public accommodation facility,
>   physical storage facility, or vehicle rental facility, or officer,
>   employee, or agent thereof, shall disclose to any person (other
>   than those officers, agents, or employees of such common carrier,
>   public accommodation facility, physical storage facility, or
>   vehicle rental facility necessary to fulfill the requirement to
>   disclose information to the Federal Bureau of Investigation under
>   this section) that the Federal Bureau of Investigation has sought
>   or obtained records pursuant to an order under this section.

The 2001 USA Patriot Act had expanded the business records provision to reach "any tangible things (including books, records, papers, documents, and other items)." Pub. L. No. 107-56, §215, 115 Stat. 272, 287. That provision, in turn, was amended by the USA Freedom Act in 2015 to regulate bulk collection in the wake of Edward Snowden's disclosures, Pub. L. No. 114-23, 129 Stat. 268 (2015), then extended to March 15, 2020. Pub. L. No. 116-69, §1703(a), 133 Stat. 1134, 1143 (2019). But after the House failed to join the Senate in extending that amendment again, the original 1998 provision went back into effect on March 15, 2020. In other words, except for then-ongoing investigations or investigations of offenses or "potential" offenses occurring before the expiration date, "business records" collection is now governed by the original 1998 standard set out above. *See* Charlie Savage, *House Departs Without Vote to Extend Expired F.B.I. Spy Tools*, N.Y. Times, Mar. 27, 2020.

Would that standard authorize an order for production of call detail records? Production of a foreign agent's personal diary? Clearly no; neither record falls within the statutory ambit. By allowing the 2020 "snapback" to the 1998 standard, Congress severely narrowed the application of the business records provision.

Would the standard authorize an order for the car rental records of a person suspected of traveling to Washington, D.C., to participate in the January 6, 2021 riot? That business record does fall within the statutory ambit: it is a record of a "vehicle rental facility." But the answer is still clearly no, because the record is not sought "for an investigation to gather foreign intelligence information or an investigation concerning international terrorism." Moreover, it seems doubtful that many (or any) of the rioters were "agent[s] of a foreign power," to whom the record must pertain.

[NSL p. 728, CTL p. 380. Insert at the end of Note 7.]

In the waning days of the Trump administration, the Justice Department reinvigorated aggressive efforts to identify the source of leaks that took place in 2017 by taking the unusual step of demanding phone and email logs of reporters from the *New York Times*, the *Washington Post*, and CNN, as well as account information regarding two members of Congress, their staffers, and members of their family from tech giants Apple and Microsoft. Justice Department policy significantly limits use of subpoenas, court orders, or warrants to obtain records from members of the media — specifying that such steps are "extraordinary measures, not standard investigatory practices"— because "freedom of the press can be no broader than the freedom of members of the news media to investigate and report the news." 28 C.F.R. §50.10(a)(1), (3) (2021). The same policy provides that if such information is sought, members of the media should receive notice unless the member of the media in question is a subject or target of an investigation. *Id.* §50.10(e). Yet neither the subjects of these requests nor the public were aware of the demands for information until June 2021, because each demand was accompanied by a nondisclosure order. *See* Jay Green, *Tech Giants Have To Hand Over Your Data When Federal Investigators Ask. Here's Why*, Wash. Post, June 15, 2021.

The debate regarding the propriety of the DOJ's efforts therefore included not only whether investigators should seek reporters' communications data in order to identify their sources, but also the legitimacy of the gag orders themselves, with media entities and First Amendment advocates seeing them as an attack on press freedom. *See, e.g.*, Charlie Savage & Kattie Benner, *U.S. Waged Secret Legal Battle to Obtain Emails of 4 Times Reporters*, N.Y. Times, June 4, 2021; Brad Smith, Opinion, *The Secret Gag Orders Must Stop*, Wash. Post, June 13, 2021. Can you think of a justification for keeping requests for such records secret? For departing from the Justice Department's normal guidelines regarding notice?

Under *Carpenter*, does the collection of large volumes of reporters' communications metadata require a warrant (as opposed to a subpoena or an 18 U.S.C. §2703(d) order, which are the tools the Justice Department is presumed to have used here)? Note that a reporter's call detail records will include not only calls to or from sources, but calls to family members, doctors, substance abuse clinics, therapists, and more. Does a comprehensive log of an individual's communications over a period of days or weeks provide a less revealing picture of that individual's private life than CSLI data do?

President Biden (who learned about the records requests and gag orders at the same time as the general public) and the Justice Department subsequently announced that the Justice Department will not seek court orders to obtain reporters' communications records to identify their sources. Eric Tucker, *Justice Department Says It'll No Longer Seize Reporter's Records During Leak Investigations*, AP, June 5, 2021. If you agree that this investigative method endangers press freedom, is that policy change a sufficient response to these revelations? If not, what would be?

[NSL p. 729, CTL p. 381. Replace Part B with the following.]

B. BULK COLLECTION OF THIRD-PARTY RECORDS

The since-expired 2001 USA Patriot Act amendment to Section 215 provided that an application for a Section 215 order from the FISC required

> a statement of facts showing that there are reasonable grounds to believe that the tangible things sought are relevant to an authorized investigation (other than a threat assessment) conducted in accordance with subsection (a)(2) of this section to obtain foreign intelligence information not concerning a United States person or to protect against international terrorism or clandestine intelligence activities. [50 U.S.C. §§1861(a)(1), (b)(2)(B).]

While it thus greatly expanded the reach of the provision, most observers believed that it would still be used for targeted collection of records about individuals.

But Edward Snowden's disclosures revealed that the NSA had used Section 215 authority for *bulk* collection of telephony metadata. In *Am. Civil Liberties Union v. Clapper*, 785 F.3d 787, 815 (2d Cir. 2015), the Second Circuit described telephony metadata and how the government used such data this way:

> Unlike what is gleaned from the more traditional investigative practice of wiretapping, telephone metadata do not include the voice content of telephone conversations. Rather, they include details about telephone calls, including, for example, the length of a call, the phone number from which the call was made, and the phone number called. Metadata can also reveal the user or device making or receiving a call through unique "identity numbers" associated with the equipment (although the government maintains that the information collected does not include information about the identities or names of individuals), and provide information about the routing of a call through the telephone network, which can sometimes (although not always) convey information about a caller's general location. . . .
>
> The government explains that it uses the bulk metadata . . . by making "queries" using metadata "identifiers" (also referred to as "selectors"), or particular phone numbers that it believes, based on "reasonable articulable suspicion," to be associated with a foreign terrorist organization. The identifier is used as a "seed" to search across the government's database; the search results yield phone numbers, and the metadata associated with them, that have been in contact with the seed. That step is referred to as the first "hop." The NSA can then also search for the numbers, and associated metadata, that have been in contact with the numbers resulting from the first search — conducting a second "hop." Until recently, the program allowed for another iteration of the process, such that a third "hop" could be conducted, sweeping in results that include the metadata of, essentially, the contacts of contacts of contacts of the original "seed." The government asserts that it does not conduct any general "browsing" of the data. . . . [*Id.* at 793-794, 797.]

See generally Nat'l Res. Council, *Bulk Collection of Signals Intelligence: Technical Options* (2015) (NSL p. 495, CTL p. 181), at 27-34. The court added, "if the orders challenged by appellants do not require the collection of metadata regarding every telephone call made or received in the United States (a point asserted by appellants and at least nominally contested by the government), they appear to come very close to doing so." *Clapper*, 785 F.3d at 815. The process might be likened to collecting a haystack to find a needle (which might or might not be located in the haystack).

The Office of the Director of National Intelligence showed how the "call event hop scenario" that the court described could generate vast numbers of "call detail records" or "CDRs":

Figure 18: **Call Event Hop Scenario and Method of Counting**

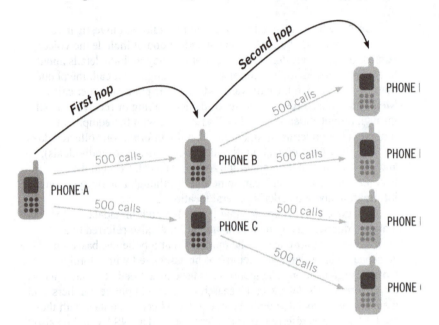

*Target uses **Phone Number A** which is the FISC-approved selector in the FISC order. This would be counted as **1 order, 1 target, 7 unique identifiers** (phone numbers A, B, C, D, E, F, G) and, assuming 500 calls between each party (1,000 records), **6000 CDRs**. CDRs may include records for both sides of a call (for example, one call from **Phone Number A** to **Phone Number B** could result in 2 records).*

ODNI, *Statistical Transparency Report Regarding the Use of National Security Authorities for Calendar Year 2018* (*ODNI Transparency Report*) (Apr. 2019).

The Snowden revelations prompted Congress to impose statutory constraints on using Section 215 for bulk collection. USA Freedom Act of 2015, Pub. L. No. 114-23, 129 Stat. 268. In the context of CDRs, the USA Freedom Act required the government to identify a "specific selection term" — a term specifically identifying a "person, account, address, or personal device" — as the basis for the production of records, where there is both reasonable grounds to believe that such CDRs are relevant to an authorized investigation (other than a threat assessment) and reasonable articulable suspicion that that term is associated with a foreign power or its agent engaged in international terrorism. 50 U.S.C.

§1861(b)(2) (2018). That authority expired with the March 15, 2020 sunset.

Notes and Questions

1. *Bulk v. Targeted Collection.* The terms "bulk" and "targeted" can be misleading. Collection using a broad identifier like "terrorism" or "Syria" is targeted, but will obviously collect a huge volume of data concerning many persons, the vast majority of whom are not persons of interest. Collecting all the traffic of a single individual is "bulk" collection if there is no other identifier. *See* Nat'l Res. Council, *supra,* at 23. The National Research Council therefore suggests this definition: "If a significant portion of the data collected is not associated with current targets, it is bulk collection; otherwise, it is targeted." *Id.* One expert speaks of the "relevance ratio — i.e., the ratio of the number of terrorist-related calls to the total number of calls on which metadata is collected." David S. Kris, *On the Bulk Collection of Tangible Things,* 7 J. Nat'l Security L. & Pol'y 209, 233 (2014). Bulk collection has a much lower relevance ratio than targeted collection. By any standard, then, the telephony metadata collection effort under Section 215 as originally enacted was bulk collection.

2. *Quantity and Quality.* Although Section 215 orders are analogous to subpoenas, bulk collection orders differ from traditional subpoenas in the quantity and quality of information they target. In *Clapper,* the government provided no information to the court to rebut the plaintiffs' claim that the government was using Section 215 to obtain *all* call detail records (and the record showed that it had at least targeted all the records held by Verizon, which handles calls for a vast number of Americans). It therefore had to admit that the quantity of records sought exceeded any quantity that had ever been associated with a grand jury subpoena. That means that the relevance ratio of a Section 215 order is orders of magnitude lower than that of any subpoena.

The quality of information collected was different, too. Can you say why from perusing the quoted definition of telephony metadata by the court in *Clapper*? How is the database that the government was compiling different from, say, business records of an entity targeted by a traditional grand jury subpoena?

3. *Relevant to What? Statutory Arguments.* Under the now-expired USA Patriot Act amendment to Section 215, the government had to provide the FISC with "a statement of facts showing that there are

reasonable grounds to believe that the tangible things sought are relevant to an authorized investigation (other than a threat assessment) conducted [under guidelines approved by the Attorney General]." 50 U.S.C. §1861(b)(2)(A). *Clapper* rejected as "unprecedented and unwarranted" the government's argument that bulk call detail records are "'relevant' because they may allow the NSA, at some unknown time in the future, utilizing its ability to sift through the trove of irrelevant data it has collected up to that point, to identify information that *is* relevant." 785 F.3d at 812; *accord United States v. Moalin*, 973 F.3d 977, 995-996 (9th Cir. 2020). *Clapper* noted that Section 215's requirement for relevance to "an authorized investigation" contemplates the "specificity of a particular investigation — not the general counterterrorism intelligence efforts of the United States government." 785 F.3d at 816. It gave the example of grand jury investigations that "are investigations of events, enterprises, or persons — the Boston Marathon bombings; Al Capone; or "Fly-by-Night Real Estate Investments," and therefore inherently "constrained by the subject of the investigation." *Id.* Did the court make the wrong comparison?

> [T]he relevant comparison may not be to any grand jury or other subpoena issued in a *single* investigation, but instead to the aggregate of subpoenas that could be or were issued in *all* of what may be thousands of specified terrorism investigations that underlie the bulk metadata collection. In a way, the bulk collection orders represent a kind of aggregation of terrorism-related collection — one-stop shopping across a potentially very large number of ongoing full or enterprise investigations. [Kris, *supra*, at 237.]

But how is this "different, in practical terms, from simply declaring that [call detail records] are relevant to counterterrorism in general"? Privacy and Civil Liberties Oversight Board, *Report on the Telephone Records Program Conducted under Section 215 of the USA PATRIOT ACT and on the Operations of the Foreign Intelligence Surveillance Court (PCLOB Report)*, Jan. 23, 2014, https://documents.pclob.gov/prod/Documents/OversightReport/ec542143-1079-424a-84b3-acc354698560/215-Report_on_the_Telephone_Records_Program.pdf. Grand jury investigations also have a finite time limit, as do the grand juries themselves. What is the time limit on the government's "counterterrorism investigation"? In fact, is the purpose of "one-stop shopping" to help any pending investigations(s), or it is chiefly to provide a database for some future investigation? *Moalin* concluded that the government's "argument depends on an after-the-fact determination of relevance: once the government had collected a massive amount of call records, it was able to find one that was relevant to a counterterrorism investigation. The problem, of course, is that FISA required the government to make a showing of relevance to a particular authorized investigation *before* collecting the records." 973 F.3d at 996.

The Foreign Intelligence Surveillance Court (FISC) disagreed with *Clapper* (and, by analogous reasoning, with *Moalin*):

> [T]here is nothing "hypothetical" or "future" about the need to conduct searches of the entire volume of records or the investigations giving rise to that need: all the records are searched to uncover contacts with numerous phone numbers or other identifiers approved under a "reasonable articulable suspicion" standard. . . . Furthermore, the tangible things are being sought in support of individual authorized investigations to protect against international terrorism and concerning various international terrorist organizations. The Court notes that tangible things are "presumptively relevant to an authorized investigation if the applicant shows in the statement of the facts that they pertain to (i) a foreign power or an agent of a foreign power; . . . or (iii) an individual in contact with, or known to, a suspected agent of a foreign power who is the subject of such authorized investigation." FISA §501(b)(2)(A). And . . . it is necessary for the government to collect telephone metadata in bulk in order to find connections between known and unknown international terrorist operatives as part of authorized investigations. [*In re Application of the Federal Bureau of Investigation*, Misc. 15-01, 2015 WL 5637562, at *8 (FISA Ct. June 29, 2015).]

Perhaps all can agree that "relevance" is not an unlimited concept and that Congress must have intended for it to impose *some* constraint on investigations. If so, what is that constraint?

At first glance, the 2021 snapback to the 1998 standard moots this debate, as it omits "relevant to" altogether, requiring just that the records be sought "for an investigation to gather foreign intelligence information or an investigation concerning international terrorism." Does "*for* an investigation" mean something different from "*relevant to* an . . . investigation"? If so, how would you articulate the limit it sets?

4. Acquisition vs. Retention and Analysis. Assuming that bulk records are digital, it is likely that they will be searched using computer algorithms and search terms. Some defenders of bulk collection have argued that people have no privacy interest in the collection of bulk digital records, because no human being initially looks at the acquired and stored data, even if it is initially filtered by computers in some crude way. *See* Richard A. Posner, Opinion, *Our Domestic Intelligence Crisis,*

Wash. Post, Dec. 21, 2005 ("[M]achine collection and processing of data cannot, as such, invade privacy. . . . [The] initial sifting [by computer], far from invading privacy (a computer is not a sentient being), keeps most private data from being read by any intelligence officer."). Privacy is first implicated at the back end of the process, they say, when human analysts examine the results.

Do you have any privacy interest in the mere acquisition and retention of your data by the government? If not, would you object to government recording of your bedroom or bathroom activities, as long as the resulting data are not analyzed? Interestingly, Congress has criminalized the mere nonconsensual *interception* of various electronic communications, as well as their disclosure. 18 U.S.C. §2511(1) (2018).

5. *The Fourth Amendment Challenge.* The FISC held that bulk collection of telephony metadata was authorized by the third-party records doctrine established by the Supreme Court's ruling in *Smith v. Maryland. In re Application of the FBI*, 2019 WL 5637562, at *9-13. Not only did it view such metadata as analogous to the numbers that Smith had called, it also thought that the quantity of call data made no difference. If each caller abandoned privacy by dialing a number, then a database of a million call details is just one million times zero — still zero. The FISC also saw no constitutionally protected privacy interest implicated in the analysis of the data either, because, under *Smith*'s reasoning, the caller voluntarily abandoned any such interest simply by using the phone to make a call.

Is this reasoning still sound after *Carpenter v. United States* (NSL p. 685, CTL p. 337)? The telephone numbers collected in *Smith* connected him to the crime, but they did not track his daily activities to create "an all-encompassing record" of his phone usage over an extended period. *Carpenter*, 138 S. Ct. at 2217. Even if the creation of telephony metadata is "voluntary" when a phone is used to make a single call, can the same be said for the creation of such data over an extended period of time? *See generally* Sharon Bradford Franklin, *Carpenter and the End of Bulk Surveillance of Americans*, Lawfare, July 25, 2018. The Ninth Circuit did not think so. In *Moalin*, it asserted (but did not decide) that the defendant's Fourth Amendment challenge to bulk collection "has considerable force," finding

> problematic . . . the extremely large number of people from whom the NSA collected telephony metadata, enabling the data to be aggregated and analyzed in bulk. . . .
>
> . . . As Amici explain, "it is relatively simple to superimpose our metadata trails onto the trails of everyone within our social group and

those of everyone within our contacts' social groups and quickly paint a picture that can be startlingly detailed" — for example, "identify[ing] the strength of relationships and the structure of organizations." Thus, the very large number of people from whom telephony metadata was collected distinguishes this case meaningfully from *Smith*. [973 F.3d at 992.]

Is the warrant requirement nevertheless excused for a different reason? In another judicial challenge to bulk collection, then-Judge Kavanaugh voted to deny rehearing of a procedural ruling by relying on *Smith v. Maryland* to conclude that the collection of telephony metadata was not a search. But even if it were, he went on, it was constitutional under the special needs exception to the Fourth Amendment. "The Government's program for bulk collection of telephony metadata serves a critically important special need — preventing terrorist attacks on the United States. In my view, that critical national security need outweighs the impact on privacy occasioned by this program." *Klayman v. Obama*, 805 F.3d 1148, 1149 (D.C. Cir. 2015) (Kavanaugh, J., concurring in denial of rehearing en banc). Would the same special needs rationale also support continuing government collection of all credit card records? If not, why not?

6. Is Bulk Collection of Telephony Metadata Useful? The 2014 PCLOB report could not identify "a single instance involving a threat to the United States in which the [Section 215] Program made a concrete difference in the outcome of a counterterrorism investigation." *PCLOB Report, supra*, at 11. The telephony metadata collected by the NSA did, however, provide additional leads regarding contacts of terrorism suspects already known to investigators or demonstrating that foreign terrorist plots do *not* have a U.S. nexus. *Id.*

7. Has Bulk Collection of Telephone Metadata (As We Know It) Ended? Even before the 2020 sunset of the bulk collection provisions of the USA Freedom Act, bulk collection — as we know it — may already have been discontinued. First, the NSA announced that it had destroyed the mass of metadata collected after the Act took effect because some telecom companies had erroneously provided it with metadata to which it was not entitled under the Act. Charlie Savage, *N.S.A. Purges Hundreds of Millions of Call and Text Records*, N.Y. Times, June 29, 2018. Second, a national security adviser for the House Minority Leader revealed that the NSA had stopped using its metadata collection authority for call detail records, *see* Robert Chesney, *Telephony Metadata: Is the Contact-Chaining Program Unsalvageable?*, Lawfare,

Mar. 5, 2019, which the Director of National Intelligence subsequently confirmed. Letter from Dan R. Coats (DNI) to Chairman Richard Burr, et al. (Aug. 14, 2019), *available at* https://int.nyt.com/data/ documenthelper/1640-odni-letter-to-congress-about/ 20bfc7d1223dba027e55/optimized/full.pdf. Third, telephony metadata may have grown increasingly less useful for investigations, as applications for alternative means of communication — including some that are encrypted end-to-end — have grown more popular.

On the other hand, does the government even need to *collect* bulk data, when it can just *buy* it from commercial database vendors? The question was recently explored by the Inspector General of the Department of Treasury in response to a congressional inquiry about the IRS Criminal Investigators' (CI) use of a commercial GPS database on a subscription basis from a vendor named Venntel. Asked about the need for warrants to use the Venntel data, the IRS responded:

> IRS-CI obtains a search warrant when conducting activity that would be considered a search under the Fourth Amendment. Before *Carpenter*, it was well-settled Supreme Court precedent that individuals could claim no legitimate expectation of privacy in information that was voluntarily turned over to a third party. With respect to the Venntel product, it is our understanding that the information available had been voluntarily turned over through individual permissions. . . . [T]he *Carpenter* decision concerned historical Cell Site Location Information which is distinct from the opt-in app data available on the Venntel platform. [Letter from J. Russell George (Inspector General, Dept. of Treasury) to Senators Ron Wyden & Elizabeth Warren, Feb. 18, 2021.]

Is the distinction the IRS draws sound? What argument can you make from *Carpenter* that phone users have a privacy interest in such GPS data? The IG commented:

> Our concern is that the Supreme Court rejected the Government's argument in *Carpenter* that CSLI is truly voluntarily provided to the phone carriers. The Court's rationale was that phone users do not truly voluntarily agree to share the information given the necessity of phones in our society. Courts may apply similar logic to GPS data sold by marketers, particularly if the Government identifies ways to translate the alphanumeric code to identify the phone's owner or has other means of identifying the phone's owner." [*Id.*]

The IG also reported, however, that "CI indicated that it is no longer using any cell phone-related data from any vendor because the data proved not to be useful in investigations." *Id.*

8. Use of NSLs. In the USA Freedom Act, Congress restricted the use of NSLs for bulk collection. For example, the authority construed in *Doe I* (NSL p. 711, CTL p. 363), was amended to provide that the Director of the FBI or his designee "may, using a term that *specifically identifies* a person, entity, telephone number, or account as the basis for a request," request the billing records and related subscriber information "relevant to an authorized investigation to protect against international terrorism . . . ." 18 U.S.C. §2709(b) (2018) (as amended by USA Freedom Act §501, 129 Stat. at 282) (emphasis added).

[NSL p. 740, CTL p. 392. Replace the Summary of Basic Principles with the following.]

THE COLLECTION AND USE OF THIRD-PARTY RECORDS: SUMMARY OF BASIC PRINCIPLES

- The government needs affirmative authority for the collection of third-party records. In the national security field, such authority is provided by statutes approving the use of national security letters (NSLs) or Section 502(a) orders to collect particular kinds of third-party records and FISA authority for pen registers and trap and trace devices, in addition to traditional authorities in criminal law.

- Most of these authorities for the collection of third-party records require that the collection be relevant to or "for" an authorized investigation to collect foreign intelligence or that it concern international terrorism — a subpoena-like standard that is more relaxed than traditional probable cause or even FISA probable cause.

- Under authorities that have since expired, the government conducted not only targeted collection of business records, but also bulk collection of both Internet and telephony metadata after 9/11.

- Courts disagreed about whether the bulk collection of telephony metadata was authorized by then-existing statutory authority or consistent with the Fourth Amendment. For example, the FISC invoked the third-party doctrine from *Smith v. Maryland* to reject a Fourth Amendment challenge to bulk collection of telephony metadata. But the Ninth Circuit was sympathetic to a similar challenge on the grounds that telephony metadata are arguably distinguishable both in quantity and quality from the telephone numbers at issue in *Smith*. (It ultimately ruled that the bulk collection at issue was not authorized by then-existing statutory authority, as had the Second Circuit in a separate case.)

- The collection and retention of bulk data by the government raises the question whether a person has a constitutionally protected privacy interest in the government's aggregation of data that has been lawfully collected under the third-party doctrine. The substantial risk of false positives in the government's use of such data also raises the question whether it should be subjected to tighter statutory regulation.

- Intelligence community lawyers have disagreed about whether the Supreme Court's reasoning in *Carpenter* applies to the government's purchase of third-party data from commercial database vendors, in light of allegedly reduced expectations of privacy in such data.

[NSL p. 754, CTL p. 406. Insert at the end of Note 4.]

In *Alasaad v. Mayorkas*, 988 F.3d 8 (1st Cir. 2021), *cert. denied*, No. 20-1505, 2021 WL 2637881 (U.S. June 28, 2021), the First Circuit said no.

> As recently explained by this circuit, *Riley* "d[id] not either create or suggest a categorical rule to the effect that the government must always secure a warrant before accessing the contents of [an electronic device]." *United States v. Rivera-Morales*, 961 F.3d 1, 14 (1st Cir. 2020). Nor does *Riley* by its own terms apply to border searches, which are entirely separate from the search incident to arrest searches discussed in *Riley*. The search incident to arrest warrant exception is premised on protecting officers and preventing evidence destruction, rather than on addressing border crime.
>
> Further, given the volume of travelers passing through our nation's borders, warrantless electronic device searches are essential to the border search exception's purpose of ensuring that the executive branch can adequately protect the border. A warrant requirement — and the delays it would incur — would hamstring the agencies' efforts to prevent border-related crime and protect this country from national security threats. [988 F.3d at 17.]

[NSL p. 756, CTL p. 408. Insert at the end of Note 6.]

The court of appeals reversed, upholding the CBP policy. *Alasaad v. Mayorkas*, 988 F.3d 8 (1st Cir. 2021), *cert. denied*, No. 20-1505, 2021 WL 2637881 (U.S. June 28, 2021).

> Electronic device searches do not fit neatly into other categories of property searches, but the bottom line is that basic border searches of electronic devices do not involve an intrusive search of a person, like the search the Supreme Court held to be non-routine in *United States v. Montoya de Hernandez*. 473 U.S. 531, 541 & n.4 (1985). Basic border searches also require an officer to manually traverse the contents of the traveler's electronic device, limiting in practice the quantity of information available during a basic search. The CBP Policy only allows searches of data resident on the device. And a basic border search does not allow government officials to view deleted or encrypted files.
>
> We thus agree with the holdings of the Ninth and Eleventh circuits that basic border searches are routine searches and need not be supported by reasonable suspicion. . . .
>
> As for advanced searches, we cannot reasonably conclude that the "substantive limitations imposed by the Constitution" on the border search exception prevent Congress from giving border agencies authority to search for information or items other than contraband. To the contrary, *Montoya de Hernandez* makes clear that the border search exception's purpose is not limited to interdicting contraband; it serves to bar entry to those "who may bring anything harmful into this country" and then gives as examples "whether that be communicable diseases, narcotics, or explosives." 473 U.S. at 544. [988 F.3d at 18-20.]

Contra United States v. Cano, 934 F.3d 1002, 1018 (9th Cir. 2019), *cert. denied*, No. 20-1043, 2021 WL 2637990 (U.S. June 28, 2021) (holding that while border searches need not be supported by reasonable suspicion, the border search exception "is restricted in scope to searches for contraband"). Given the square disagreement between the First and Ninth Circuits, is it odd that the Supreme Court would allow such a circuit split to persist?

––––––––––––

[NSL p. 771, CTL p. 423. Insert before the last sentence of Note 3.]

Elhady was reversed on appeal. *Elhady v. Kable*, 993 F.3d 208 (4th Cir. 2021). First, the court stressed that the plaintiffs' facial challenge to their inclusion on the Selectee List for enhanced screening at airports required the court to consider the "average" delay or injury, not the "outlier." *Id.* at 218. It complained that "[f]acial challenges are . . . not well suited to the multiple layers of sensitivity that surround this case. Plaintiffs come before us with wildly varying circumstances and ask for a common remedy." *Id.* at 225. Notwithstanding plaintiffs' allegations of some outliers, the court found the *average* delay experienced by plaintiffs was an hour or less, *id.* at 223, and that no plaintiff was prevented from taking a later flight (none were on the No-Fly List) or alternative transportation. *Id.* at 222 (declaring somewhat cavalierly that "[a]lthough our law may guarantee the citizen's right to travel, it is less attentive to how he gets there."). Second, because the average effect of selection for enhanced screening was relatively trivial, the court reasoned that plaintiffs had shown no "plus" factor reaching the "stigma-plus" threshold for a protected interest under the Fifth Amendment. *Id.* at 226-227. The court thus joined the Tenth and Sixth Circuits in concluding that the challenge to selection for and application of enhanced screening implicated no constitutionally protected interests. *See Abdi v. Wray,* 942 F.3d 1019 (10th Cir. 2019); *Beydoun v. Sessions,* 871 F.3d 459 (6th Cir. 2017).

Although the court therefore did not need to conduct a due process balancing of interests, it expressed serious doubt in dicta that such balancing would favor the plaintiffs in light of the strong federal security interest and the "comparatively weak" weight of the private interests. *Elhady,* 993 F.3d at 228.

[NSL p. 774, CTL p. 426. Insert before the last sentence of Note 7.]

The Fourth Circuit disagreed. It found that disclosure by one government agency to another was not "public disclosure" by the government. *Elhady v. Kable,* 993 F.3d 208, 225-226 (4th Cir. 2021). Moreover, the court agreed with the Tenth Circuit that "the government's act of including names in the TSDB does not *mandate* that private entities deny people such [employment] privileges. It merely makes information available to private entities, like companies handling nuclear power, and then those companies make their own choices." *Id.* at 227. It found that plaintiffs had not shown that disclosure to employers had led to any employment-related injury.

[NSL p. 818, CTL p. 470. Insert at the end of Note 7.]

Citing mootness, the Sixth Circuit dismissed the appeal in *Arab American Civil Rights League,* and remanded to the district court to dismiss the case without prejudice. *Arab Am. Civil Rights League v. Trump,* No. 19-2375, 2021 U.S. App. LEXIS 3754 (6th Cir. Feb. 10, 2021) (mem.).

After *Trump,* a district court in *IRAP* again denied in part the government's motion to dismiss. *Int'l Refugee Assistance Project v. Trump,* 373 F. Supp. 3d 650 (D. Md.), *motion to certify appeal granted,* 404 F. Supp. 3d 946 (D. Md. 2019), and *rev'd and remanded,* 961 F.3d 635 (4th Cir. 2020). On an interlocutory appeal by the government, the Fourth Circuit found no room in the Supreme Court's opinion to sustain the denial.

> [E]very reason that the *Hawaii* Court gave to reach its conclusion applies here. Yet, despite the Supreme Court's clear and unambiguous conclusion about the justification for Proclamation 9645, the district court in this case concluded that the plaintiffs had plausibly alleged that the same Proclamation reflected *no* legitimate purpose. In doing so, it erred as a matter of law. Therefore, even to the extent that the plaintiffs' constitutional claims are subject to rational basis review, rather than the *Mandel* standard, the district court should have dismissed them for failing to state a claim to relief that is plausible on its face. [961 F.3d at 653.]

[NSL p. 818, CTL p. 470. Insert after Note 8.]

Proclamation on Ending Discriminatory Bans on Entry to the United States

86 Fed. Reg. 7005 (Jan. 25, 2021)

The United States was built on a foundation of religious freedom and tolerance, a principle enshrined in the United States Constitution. Nevertheless, the previous administration enacted a number of Executive Orders and Presidential Proclamations that prevented certain individuals from entering the United States — first from primarily Muslim countries, and later, from largely African countries. Those actions are a stain on our national conscience and are inconsistent with our long history of welcoming people of all faiths and no faith at all.

Beyond contravening our values, these Executive Orders and Proclamations have undermined our national security. They have jeopardized our global network of alliances and partnerships and are a moral blight that has dulled the power of our example the world over. And they have separated loved ones, inflicting pain that will ripple for years to come. They are just plain wrong.

Make no mistake, where there are threats to our Nation, we will address them. Where there are opportunities to strengthen information-sharing with partners, we will pursue them. And when visa applicants request entry to the United States, we will apply a rigorous, individualized vetting system. But we will not turn our backs on our values with discriminatory bans on entry into the United States.

NOW, THEREFORE, I, JOSEPH R. BIDEN JR., President of the United States, by the authority vested in me by the Constitution and the laws of the United States of America, including sections 212(f) and 215(a) of the Immigration and Nationality Act, 8 U.S.C. 1182(f) and 1185(a), hereby find that it is in the interests of the United States to revoke Executive Order 13780 of March 6, 2017 (Protecting the Nation From Foreign Terrorist Entry Into the United States), Proclamation 9645 of September 24, 2017 (Enhancing Vetting Capabilities and Processes for Detecting Attempted Entry Into the United States by Terrorists or Other Public-Safety Threats), Proclamation 9723 of April 10, 2018 (Maintaining Enhanced Vetting Capabilities and Processes for Detecting Attempted Entry Into the United States by Terrorists or Other Public-Safety Threats), and Proclamation 9983 of January 31, 2020 (Improving Enhanced Vetting Capabilities and Processes for

Detecting Attempted Entry Into the United States by Terrorists or Other Public-Safety Threats). Our national security will be enhanced by revoking the Executive Order and Proclamations.

Accordingly, I hereby proclaim:

Section 1. Revocations. Executive Order 13780, and Proclamations 9645, 9723, and 9983 are hereby revoked. . . .

[Subsequent sections resume visa processing consistent with the revocation and direct review of information-sharing relationships.]

Joseph R. Biden, Jr.

[NSL p. 862, CTL p. 514. Insert after Note 3.]

3a. The Supreme Court Narrows the Scope of the Suspension Clause. In *Dep't of Homeland Security* v. *Thuraissigiam*, 140 S. Ct. 1959 (2020), the Supreme Court sidestepped the issue that had divided the Third and Ninth Circuits (whether the Suspension Clause applied to undocumented immigrants physically but not lawfully present within the United States) in favor of a different — and perhaps more significant conclusion. Writing for a five-Justice majority, Justice Alito held that the habeas review protected by the Suspension Clause did *not* include challenges by non-citizens to final orders of removal — because such challenges did not contest the legality of the detainee's underlying confinement, but rather sought to block his removal from the country. *See id.* at 1968-1971. Concurring in the judgment, Justice Breyer (joined by Justice Ginsburg) would have resolved the case on the narrower grounds that the Respondent was an undocumented immigrant arrested shortly after entering the country without authorization, and that his substantive claims were entirely a creature of statute. *Id.* at 1988-1993 (Breyer, J., concurring in the judgment). And Justice Sotomayor (joined by Justice Kagan) wrote a lengthy and impassioned dissent, arguing that the Constitution did indeed apply to — and required meaningful review of — the Respondent's claims. *Id.* at 1993-2015 (Sotomayor, J., dissenting). Although *Thuraissigiam* ducked the question of whether undocumented immigrants physically present in the United States are protected by the Suspension Clause, its holding may have *broader* implications — as it marks the first time that the Supreme Court explicitly held that a class of substantive claims by detainees held inside the United States (here, challenges to removal orders) is not protected by the Constitution. What implications might this have for Congress's power to bar federal courts from entertaining *other* claims brought by those subject to executive detention? Does *Thuraissigiam* suggest that the Suspension Clause does not extend to challenges to conditions of confinement? Challenges to the jurisdiction of military commissions? Even if *Thuraissigiam* can be reconciled with the bottom-line holdings in *Boumediene*, does this suggest tension with Justice Kennedy's discussion of the role of the habeas writ?

[NSL p. 916, CTL p. 568. Insert after Note 2.]

2a. Al-Hela and the Laws of War. The D.C. Circuit did not return to the issue resolved (and then dicta-ized) in *Al-Bihani* until 2020. In *Al-Hela v. Trump*, 972 F.3d 120 (D.C. Cir. 2020), a three-judge panel upheld the detention of a Yemeni national on the ground that he had provided "substantial support" to Al Qaeda and associated forces because "[i]n the years leading up to [his] disappearance and detention, terrorist leaders relied on Al Hela to transport fighters within Yemen and across regional borders in furtherance of attacks against the United States and its allies, including by leveraging his government contacts to procure fake identification and travel documents." *Id.* at 129.

In reaching that conclusion, the panel rejected Al-Hela's argument that detention based on "substantial support" requires the government to show that he was *actually* involved in hostilities against the United States. Reincorporating the *Al-Bihani* panel's (contested) discussion of the relationship between the AUMF and the laws of war, the *Al-Hela* panel also read the FY2012 NDAA to not require such a relationship — even though that statute expressly authorizes the United States "to detain covered persons . . . pending disposition under the law of war" (casebook p. 905). *See Al-Hela*, 972 F.3d at 129-132. "In recognition of the global and diffuse nature of the conflict," Judge Rao wrote for the panel, the AUMF and NDAA's detention authority "covers not only those who are part of covered terrorist organizations or directly aid hostilities, but also those who substantially support the organizations by facilitating the logistics and planning that make their activities possible." *Id.* at 135. The panel also rejected Al-Hela's substantive and procedural due process challenges to his detention — with two of the three judges holding the Due Process Clause inapplicable to Guantánamo detainees. *See id.* at 135-150. *But see id.* at 151-155 (Griffith, J., concurring in part and concurring in the judgment) (explaining that it was unnecessary for the panel to decide whether the Due Process Clause applies to Guantánamo detainees).

On April 23, 2021, the D.C. Circuit granted Al-Hela's petition for rehearing en banc and vacated the panel's judgment. But the order granting rehearing (and setting argument for September 30, 2021) directed the parties "to limit briefing to the question of whether [Al-Hela] is entitled to relief on his claims under the Due Process Clause." *Al-Hela v. Biden*, No. 19-5079, Order at 2 (D.C. Cir. Apr. 23, 2021) (en banc). If that means that the en banc court is *not* going to revisit the panel's interpretation of "substantial support" or the more general relationship between the NDAA and the laws of war, then the panel decision could have enormous ramifications (at least on these issues) going forward. Indeed, shortly after the order granting rehearing en banc, the D.C. Circuit suspending briefing in a different detainee's appeal of a district court decision that had also relied entirely on "substantial support" as the basis for detention. *See Paracha v. Trump*, 453 F. Supp. 3d 168 (D.D.C. 2020), *appeal docketed*, No. 20-5039 (D.C. Cir.).

[NSL p. 920, CTL p. 572. Insert at the end of Note 2.]

As noted immediately above in this *Supplement*, the D.C. Circuit in *Al-Hela v. Trump*, 972 F.3d 120 (D.C. Cir. 2020), adopted a remarkably broad definition of "substantial support," and one that did not turn on whether the conduct met the threshold for belligerency under the laws of war. It's worth reflecting on how that holding, had it been on the books in 2013, might have affected the Second Circuit's analysis in *Hedges*. If "substantial support" under the FY2012 NDAA includes "those who substantially support [Al Qaeda and affiliated groups] by facilitating the logistics and planning that make their activities possible," *id.* at 135, isn't there a much stronger argument that at least some of the plaintiffs in *Hedges* had Article III standing?

[NSL p. 932, CTL p. 584. Insert after Note 2.]

3. Al-Hela and the Due Process Debate. As noted in Note 2, the D.C. Circuit in *Qassim v. Trump*, 927 F.3d 522 (D.C. Cir. 2019), went out of its way to clarify that, as of 2019, there was no binding D.C. Circuit precedent resolving, one way or the other, whether (and to what extent) the Guantánamo detainees were protected by the Due Process Clause. In *Al-Hela v. Trump*, 972 F.3d 120 (D.C. Cir. 2020), two judges on a three-judge panel emphatically held that the Due Process Clause does *not* apply to Guantánamo detainees. Writing for herself and Judge Randolph (who wrote the D.C. Circuit's decisions in *Rasul, Hamdan, Boumediene, Kiyemba,* and *Al-Adahi*), Judge Rao rejected both Al-Hela's "substantive challenge to his detention and several "procedural" challenges to the rules governing his habeas case on the ground that "it would be well beyond our authority to extend or to create new constitutional limits on the conduct of wartime detention by the political branches." *Id.* at 143. Relying on *Johnson v. Eisentrager,* 339 U.S. 763 (1950), and distinguishing *Boumediene v. Bush,* 553 U.S. 723 (2008), the *Al-Hela* panel found the due process question "readily answered by existing precedent." *Id.* at 147. Among other things, the panel's due process holding was thus fatal to Al-Hela's argument that, even if his detention was initially lawful, its duration violated due process. *See also Ali v. Trump,* 959 F.3d 364 (D.C. Cir. 2020) (holding, before *Al-Hela,* that even if the Due Process Clause applied, it did not impose a durational limit on a Guantánamo detainee's confinement).

Concurring in part and concurring in the judgment, Judge Griffith would have avoided the question of whether the Due Process Clause applies *at all* by holding that it was satisfied in Al-Hela's case. As Griffith wrote, "Al Hela's challenge to the length of his detention fails under established case law, regardless of whether he may bring that challenge under the Due Process Clause in the first place. And his three procedural challenges fail under our precedent developed under the Suspension Clause in the wake of *Boumediene.* That precedent provides Al Hela as much process as he would have been due under the Due Process Clause with respect to his particular claims." *Id.* at 151 (Griffith, J., concurring in part and concurring in the judgment).

On April 23, 2021, the D.C. Circuit agreed to rehear en banc "whether [Al-Hela] is entitled to relief on his claims under the Due Process Clause." *Al-Hela v. Biden,* No. 19-5079, Order at 2 (D.C. Cir. Apr. 23, 2021) (en banc). Thus, the full D.C. Circuit appears poised to (finally) answer whether (and to what extent) the Due Process Clause applies to Guantánamo detainees. But does Judge Griffith's concurrence give the full court a pathway to avoiding that question? The answer presumably depends on whether a majority of the court's active judges *agree* with Judge Griffith that the judge-made rules surveyed in this chapter provide Guantánamo detainees with all the process that the Constitution requires. Given what you've read and discussed in these materials, especially the analyses in *Al-Bihani, Al-Adahi,* and *Latif,* do *you* agree with Judge Griffith on this point? Why or why not? Either way, wouldn't it be useful for the full court to finally settle, one way or the other, what role constitutional due process has to play in the Guantánamo cases?

[NSL p. 958, CTL p. 610. Insert at the end of Note 5.]

After the evidentiary hearing, the district court ruled in June 2020 that Hassoun's detention was unlawful, largely because the government was *unable* to make the factual showing required by Section 412 to justify detention. The court thereby sidestepped Hassoun's constitutional challenge to Section 412. *See Hassoun v. Searls*, 469 F. Supp. 3d 69 (W.D.N.Y. 2020). Although the district court refused to stay its decision, the Second Circuit issued a stay — not because it thought the government was likely to prevail on the Section 412 issue (indeed, only the D.C. Circuit can hear appeals of habeas petitions challenging detention under Section 412), but because it thought the government was likely to prevail on a *different* basis for detention that the district court had rejected months earlier. *See Hassoun v. Searls*, 968 F.3d 190 (2d Cir. 2020). Perhaps reflecting its lack of confidence in the merits of its case, the government, which had spent years arguing that there was no country to which Hassoun could be removed, finally effectuated his removal on July 22, 2020 (according to news reports, to Rwanda — where he was granted asylum). Thus, by the time the Second Circuit issued its ruling (on July 30, 2020), Hassoun had already been free for eight days — mooting both his habeas petition and the government's appeal. Curiously, the Second Circuit granted the *government*'s subsequent request to vacate the adverse district court ruling (that the Court of Appeals' July 30 ruling stayed), but denied Hassoun's request to vacate *its* July 30 ruling — even though the case was clearly moot by then. *See Hassoun v. Searls*, 976 F.3d 121 (2d Cir. 2020).

The Second Circuit's inconsistent behavior notwithstanding, the key for present purposes is that, by removing Hassoun and mooting his case, the government (1) avoided an appellate ruling on the scope of Section 412, and (2) succeeded in wiping off the books the district court's holding that the government had failed to meet its factual burden in Hassoun's case.

[NSL p. 1023, CTL p. 675. Add at the end of the first paragraph, p. 1023.]

CACI's petition for certiorari was denied on June 28, 2021 — shortly after *Nestlé USA, Inc. v. Doe*, 141 S. Ct. 1931 (2021), further clarified the scope of the Alien Tort Statute. *See CACI Premier Tech., Inc. v. Al Shimari*, No. 19-648, 2021 WL 2637838 (U.S. June 28, 2021) (mem.).

[NSL p. 1027, CTL p. 679. Add after Note 4.d.]

e. *U.S. Efforts to Block Foreign Investigations of U.S. Involvement in Torture.* After the ECHR ruled in Abu Zubaydah's favor in 2014, finding that Poland knew of the CIA activities on its territory, Poland resumed its criminal investigation, enabling Abu Zubaydah to submit evidence to the Polish courts. He then sought to subpoena evidence in the United States of his detention and torture, including testimony from former CIA contractors James Mitchell and John "Bruce" Jessen, pursuant to 28 U.S.C. §1782(a), which authorizes federal district courts to order discovery for use in litigation outside the United States. When the district court granted the discovery request and Mitchell and Jessen were subpoenaed, the United States intervened and invoked the state secrets privilege in an effort to quash the subpoenas. The district court then ruled in the government's favor, and a divided Ninth Circuit panel reversed, finding that some of the information sought by the subpoenas was not subject to the privilege because it was "public knowledge." *Husayn v. Mitchell*, 938 F.3d 1123 (9th Cir. 2019).

In April 2021, the Supreme Court granted the government's petition for a writ of certiorari to review the Ninth Circuit decision. *See United States v. Zubaydah*, No. 20-827, 2021 WL 1602639 (U.S. Apr. 26, 2021) (mem.); *see also* Rohini Kurup, *Supreme Court to Hear State Secrets Case Involving Guantanamo Detainee*, Lawfare, June 10, 2021; Adam Liptak & Carol Rosenberg, *Supreme Court to Rule on Whether C.I.A. Black Sites Are State Secrets*, N.Y Times, Apr. 26, 2021. The case is scheduled for oral argument on Wednesday, October 6, 2021.

[NSL p. 1032, CTL p. 684. Insert after the first paragraph.]

The January 6, 2021, riot at the Capitol instantaneously redirected the focus of "criminalizing terrorism." Now the threat is seen as coming also from within, prompting hot debate about the definition of "domestic terrorism" and the adequacy of existing criminal laws and investigative priorities and policies. This was the intelligence community's assessment of that threat in March 2021:

National Strategy for Countering Domestic Terrorism
pp. 10-11, June 2021

The Intelligence Community (IC) assesses that domestic violent extremists (DVEs) who are motivated by a range of ideologies and galvanized by recent political and societal events in the United States pose an elevated threat to the Homeland in 2021. Enduring DVE motivations pertaining to biases against minority populations and perceived government overreach will almost certainly continue to drive DVE radicalization and mobilization to violence. Newer sociopolitical developments — such as narratives of fraud in the recent general election, the emboldening impact of the violent breach of the U.S. Capitol, conditions related to the COVID-19 pandemic, and conspiracy theories promoting violence — will almost certainly spur some DVEs to try to engage in violence this year.

The IC assesses that lone offenders or small cells of DVEs adhering to a diverse set of violent extremist ideologies are more likely to carry out violent attacks in the Homeland than organizations that allegedly advocate a DVE ideology. DVE attackers often radicalize independently by consuming violent extremist material online and mobilize without direction from a violent extremist organization, making detection and disruption difficult.

The IC assesses that racially or ethnically motivated violent extremists (RMVEs) and militia violent extremists (MVEs) present the most lethal DVE threats, with RMVEs most likely to conduct mass-casualty attacks against civilians and MVEs typically targeting law enforcement and government personnel and facilities. The IC assesses that the MVE threat increased last year and that it will almost certainly continue to be elevated throughout 2021 because of contentious sociopolitical factors that motivate MVEs to commit violence.

The IC assesses that U.S. RMVEs who promote the superiority of the white race are the DVE actors with the most persistent and concerning transnational connections because individuals with similar ideological beliefs exist outside of the United States and these RMVEs frequently communicate with and seek to influence each other. We assess that a small number of US RMVEs have traveled abroad to network with like-minded individuals.

The IC assesses that DVEs exploit a variety of popular social media platforms, smaller websites with targeted audiences, and encrypted chat applications to recruit new adherents, plan and rally support for in-person actions, and disseminate materials that contribute to radicalization and mobilization to violence.

The IC assesses that several factors could increase the likelihood or lethality of DVE attacks in 2021 and beyond, including escalating support from persons in the United States or abroad, growing perceptions of government overreach related to legal or policy changes and disruptions, and high-profile attacks spurring follow-on attacks and innovations in targeting and attack tactics.

DVE lone offenders will continue to pose significant detection and disruption challenges because of their capacity for independent radicalization to violence, ability to mobilize discretely, and access to firearms.

See also Off. of the Dir. of Nat'l Intelligence, *Domestic Violent Extremism Poses Heightened Threat in 2021* (Mar. 1, 2021); Robert O'Harrow Jr., Andrew Ba Tran & Derek Hawkins, *The Rise in Domestic Extremism in America*, Wash. Post, Apr. 12, 2021 (reporting that since 2015, right-wing extremists have been involved in 267 plots or attacks causing 91 fatalities, while left-wing extremists accounted for 66 incidents causing 19 fatalities).

At this writing, a massive and intense investigation of the January 6 riot is still ongoing. *See, e.g.*, Drew Harwell & Craig Timberg, *How America's Surveillance Networks Helped the FBI Catch the Capitol Mob*, Wash. Post, Apr. 2, 2021. Almost 400 people have been charged with criminal offenses so far. *See, e.g.*, Rebecca Harrington, *300 People Have Been Charged in the Capitol Insurrection So Far*, Insider, Mar. 31, 2021. Most charges have been misdemeanor charges (often involving trespassing). But more than 100 are felony charges for assaulting a federal officer, and 25 are for conspiracy. *See, e.g.*, Clare Hynes, Cassidy McDonald, & Eleanor Watson, *What We Know About the "Unprecedented" Capitol Riot Arrests*, CBS News, Apr. 1, 2021; Kyle Cheney, *Many Capitol Rioters Unlikely to Serve Jail Time*, Politico, Mar. 30, 2021.

[NSL p. 1033, CTL p. 685. Insert after Case Study.]

Several defendants in the Unite the Right "Rally" case pleaded conditionally guilty to violating the Anti-Riot Act, 18 U.S.C. §§2101-2102, subject to their right to appeal its constitutionality. That appeal resulted in the following opinion:

United States v. Miselis

United States Court of Appeals, Fourth Circuit, 2020
972 F.3d 518, *cert. denied*, No. 20-1241, 2021 WL 2405168
(U.S. June 14, 2021)

Before KING, DIAZ, and RUSHING, Circuit Judges.

DIAZ, Circuit Judge: Michael Paul Miselis and Benjamin Drake
Daley entered conditional guilty pleas to one count each of conspiracy to
commit an offense against the United States, in violation of 18 U.S.C.
§371, with the substantive offense being a violation of the Anti-Riot Act,
18 U.S.C. §§2101-02. The charges arise from the defendants' violent
participation in three white supremacist rallies during the year 2017: two
in their home state of California, and the third being the notorious "Unite
the Right" rally in Charlottesville, Virginia.

On appeal, the defendants challenge their convictions on the grounds
that the Anti-Riot Act is facially overbroad under the Free Speech Clause
of the First Amendment, as well as void for vagueness under the Due
Process Clause of the Fifth Amendment. Reviewing these issues de novo,
we disagree that the statute is unconstitutionally vague. But we agree that
it treads too far upon constitutionally protected speech — in *some* of its
applications. . . .

In all other respects, however, the statute comports with the First
Amendment. And because the discrete instances of overbreadth are
severable from the remainder of the statute, the appropriate remedy is to
invalidate the statute only to the extent that it reaches too far, while
leaving the remainder intact.

Finally, because the factual bases for the defendants' guilty pleas
conclusively establish that their own substantive offense conduct —
which involves *no* First Amendment activity — falls under the Anti-Riot
Act's surviving applications, their convictions stand.

I.

We begin with an overview of the defendants' offense conduct, the
procedural history, and the Anti-Riot Act. . . .

C.

Congress passed the Anti-Riot Act as a rider to the Civil Rights Act
of 1968, amidst an era, not unlike our own, marked by a palpable degree
of social unrest. *See* Anti-Riot Act, Pub. L. No. 90-284 §104(a), 82 Stat.

73, 75-77 (April 11, 1968). The statute's passage followed on the heels of what has been deemed the "long, hot summer of 1967," in which more than 150 cities across 34 states witnessed riots stirred by issues such as racial injustice and the war in Vietnam. *See generally* Malcolm McLaughlin, The Long, Hot Summer of 1967: Urban Rebellion in America (2014). And the statute's immediate catalyst was the upheaval sparked anew, in over 100 American cities, by the assassination of Martin Luther King, Jr. on April 4, 1968. *See* Marvin Zalman, *The Federal Anti-Riot Act and Political Crime: The Need for Criminal Law Theory*, 20 Vill. L. Rev. 897, 912 (1975). . . .

The Anti-Riot Act comprises three provisions that bear on the defendants' facial challenges: one that proscribes a range of speech and conduct, and two that contribute to the definition of such speech and conduct. *First* and foremost, §2101(a) provides that:

> Whoever travels in interstate or foreign commerce or uses any facility of interstate or foreign commerce, including, but not limited to, the mail, telegraph, telephone, radio, or television, with intent —
>
> > (1) to incite a riot; or
> > (2) to organize, promote, encourage, participate in, or carry on a riot; or
> > (3) to commit any act of violence in furtherance of a riot; or
> > (4) to aid or abet any person in inciting or participating in or carrying on a riot or committing any act of violence in furtherance of a riot;
>
> and who either during the course of any such travel or use or thereafter performs or attempts to perform any other overt act for any purpose specified in subparagraph (A), (B), (C), or (D) of this paragraph —
>
> Shall be fined under this title, or imprisoned not more than five years, or both.

18 U.S.C. §2101(a).

Second, §2102(a) defines the "riot" at the center of the statute, and which forms the object of §2101(a)'s laundry list of alternative purposes, to mean

> a public disturbance involving (1) an act or acts of violence by one or more persons part of an assemblage of three or more persons, which act or acts shall constitute a clear and present danger of, or shall result in, damage or injury to the property of any other person or to the person of

any other individual or (2) a threat or threats of the commission of an act or acts of violence by one or more persons part of an assemblage of three or more persons having, individually or collectively, the ability of immediate execution of such threat or threats, where the performance of the threatened act or acts of violence would constitute a clear and present danger of, or would result in, damage or injury to the property of any other person or to the person of any other individual.

Id. §2102(a).

And *third*, §2102(b) glosses the ordinary meaning of each of the speech- and conduct-related verbs found in §2101(a)(1)-(2) as follows:

As used in this chapter, the term "to incite a riot", or "to organize, promote, encourage, participate in, or carry on a riot", includes, but is not limited to, urging or instigating other persons to riot, but shall not be deemed to mean the mere oral or written (1) advocacy of ideas or (2) expression of belief, not involving advocacy of any act or acts of violence or assertion of the rightness of, or the right to commit, any such act or acts.

Id. §2102(b). Because the statute's constitutionality hinges on these three interlocking provisions, we focus on them as we address the defendants' appeal. . . .

III. . . .

A.

We begin by setting out the principles that guide our overbreadth analysis. Here, the defendants bring a facial challenge to the Anti-Riot Act, meaning they claim that the statute is unconstitutional *not* as it applies to their own conduct, but rather "on its face," as it applies to the population generally. *See Wash. State Grange v. Wash. State Republican Party*, 552 U.S. 442, 449 (2008). Such claims of facial invalidity "are disfavored for several reasons." *Id.* at 450 (cleaned up). For one thing, facial challenges "run contrary to the fundamental principle of judicial restraint that courts should neither anticipate a question of constitutional law in advance of the necessity of deciding it nor formulate a rule of constitutional law that is broader than is required by the precise facts to which it is to be applied." *Id.* (cleaned up). Relatedly, facial challenges "threaten to short circuit the democratic process by preventing laws embodying the will of the people from being implemented in a manner consistent with the Constitution." *Id.* at 451.

In light of these twin concerns, a facial challenge typically requires a showing that "no set of circumstances exists under which the Act would be valid, *i.e.*, that the law is unconstitutional in all of its applications," *Wash. State Grange*, 552 U.S. at 449 (cleaned up); or "that the statute lacks any plainly legitimate sweep," *United States v. Stevens*, 559 U.S. 460, 472 (2010) (cleaned up). And in assessing whether a statute meets one of these high bars, courts must typically take care "not to . . . speculate about hypothetical or imaginary cases." *Wash. State Grange*, 552 U.S. at 450 (cleaned up).

In the First Amendment context, however, the fear of chilling protected expression "has led courts to entertain facial challenges based merely on hypothetical applications of the law to nonparties." *Preston v. Leake*, 660 F.3d 726, 738 (4th Cir. 2011). Under this "second type" of facial challenge, a statute "may be invalidated as overbroad" as long as "a substantial number of its applications are unconstitutional, judged in relation to the statute's plainly legitimate sweep." *Stevens*, 559 U.S. at 473 (cleaned up). . . .

Overbreadth analysis proceeds along several steps. Because "it is impossible to determine whether a statute reaches too far without first knowing what the statute covers," we must first "construe the challenged statute." [*United States v. Williams*, 553 U.S. 285, 293 (2008)]. In so doing, we must seek to avoid any "constitutional problems" by asking whether the statute is "subject to [ ] a limiting construction." *New York v. Ferber*, 458 U.S. 747, 769 n.24 (1982). We must then determine whether, so construed, the statute "criminalizes a substantial amount of protected expressive activity." *Williams*, 553 U.S. at 297. Finally, if the statute proves "impermissibly overbroad," we must assess whether "the unconstitutional portion" is "severable" from the remainder; if so, only that portion "is to be invalidated." *Ferber*, 458 U.S. at 769 n.24. Altogether, these efforts to preserve a statute from facial invalidation reflect the notion "that the overbreadth doctrine is strong medicine," to be applied "only as a last resort," in cases where it is "truly warranted." *See id.* at 769.

In conducting our analysis, we find it preferable, at least in the context of the Anti-Riot Act, to begin (at step zero, as it were) by delineating the scope of unprotected speech that the statute aims to regulate. *Cf.* [*United States v. Dellinger*, 472 F.2d 340, 358 (7th Cir. 1972)] ("Ideally the analysis should begin with a delineation of the scope of speech protected by the first amendment."). With that backdrop in mind, we'll be better able to perceive where the statute overshoots its target and purports to regulate a substantial amount of *protected* speech.

B.

A glance at the Anti-Riot Act reveals that the category of unprotected speech that lies at the core of the statute's prohibition is that which also lies at the origin of First Amendment jurisprudence: "incitement." In general legal parlance, "incitement" refers to "[t]he act of persuading" — that is, of inducing — "another person to commit a crime." *See Incitement*, Black's Law Dictionary (11th ed. 2019); *cf. Persuade*, Black's Law Dictionary (11th ed. 2019) ("To induce (another) to do something; to make someone decide to do something[.]"). More important for our purposes is how the Supreme Court has defined "incitement" in First Amendment jurisprudence. And notably, while the Court initially did so much more broadly than the dictionary, the modern test does so almost as narrowly.

The modern incitement test derives from the Court's per curiam decision in *Brandenburg* [v. *Ohio*], 395 U.S. 444, which came down in 1969, the year *after* the Anti-Riot Act was enacted. That case concerned the conviction of a Ku Klux Klan leader under the Ohio Criminal Syndicalism statute, *id.* at 444-45, which made it a crime to "advocate or teach the duty, necessity, or propriety of violence as a means of accomplishing industrial or political reform," *id.* at 448 (cleaned up).[5]

Though the Court had upheld an analogous statute in *Whitney v. California*, 274 U.S. 357 (1927), it asserted that *Whitney* "ha[d] been thoroughly discredited by later decisions," from which it distilled the principle that "the constitutional guarantees of free speech" protected the "advocacy of the use of force or of law violation except where such advocacy is directed to inciting or producing imminent lawless action and is likely to incite or produce such action." *See id.* at 447. And because the Ohio statute "purport[ed] to punish *mere* advocacy" of lawless action as opposed to advocacy *directed* and *likely* to produce *imminent* lawless action, the Court held that it fell "within the condemnation" of the First Amendment. *Id.* at 449 (emphasis added). . . .

Brandenburg has thus been widely understood . . . as having significantly (if tacitly) narrowed the category of incitement. These days . . . advocacy of lawlessness retains the guarantees of free speech unless it's directed and likely to produce imminent lawlessness.

---

5. The specific words giving rise to the Klansman's prosecution in *Brandenburg* were these: "We're not a revengent organization, but if our President, our Congress, our Supreme Court, continues to suppress the white, Caucasian race, it's possible that there might have to be some revengeance taken." *See id.* at 446.

As a corollary, we've understood *Brandenburg*'s protection to be limited to *mere* or "abstract" advocacy. *Rice v. Paladin Enters., Inc.*, 128 F.3d 233, 243 (4th Cir. 1997); *cf. Brandenburg*, 395 U.S. at 447-48 ("[T]he mere abstract teaching of the moral propriety . . . [of] a resort to force and violence[ ] is not the same as preparing a group for violent action and steeling it to such action." (cleaned up)). Speech taking some form "other than abstract advocacy," by contrast, such as that which "constitutes . . . aiding and abetting of criminal conduct," doesn't implicate the First Amendment under our *Rice* decision. *See* 128 F.3d at 239, 242-43 (holding that the publication of a *Hit Man: A Technical Manual for Independent Contractors*, whose detailed and concrete instructions on "how to murder and become a professional killer" assisted a man in taking three lives, wasn't protected abstract advocacy); *see also Williams*, 553 U.S. at 299–300 (suggesting that *Brandenburg* only protects "abstract advocacy"). In other words, *Rice* effectively recognizes a second category of unprotected speech inherent in that of incitement, which may be proscribed without regard to whether it's directed and likely to produce imminent lawlessness.

With this delineation in mind, we consider whether the Anti-Riot Act encompasses the sort of advocacy that *Brandenburg* "jealously protects." *See Rice*, 128 F.3d at 262. . . .

C.

We find it useful to begin our analysis of the Anti-Riot Act by breaking §2101(a) down into the four essential elements of a violation, which are:

> (1) "travel[ing] in . . . or us[ing] any facility of interstate commerce";
> (2) "with intent" either to a) "incite"; b) "organize, promote, encourage, participate in, or carry on"; c) "commit any act of violence in furtherance of"; or d) "aid or abet any person in inciting or participating in or carrying on . . . or committing any act of violence in furtherance of";
> (3) "a riot"; and
> (4) "perform[ing] or attempt[ing] to perform any other overt act," for any of the foregoing purposes, "either during the course of any such travel or use or thereafter."

See 18 U.S.C. §2101(a). Stated otherwise, a violation requires two overt acts plus specific intent to carry out one or more of numerous alternative purposes with respect to a riot.

The defendants argue that three of these elements tread on protected advocacy: (1) the "any other" (or second, in addition to the antecedent "travel in . . . or use of any facility of interstate commerce") overt act element; (2) the specific-intent element; and (3) the definition of a "riot." We construe the statute by focusing on each in turn.

1.

We start with the defendants' contention that the "any other" or second overt-act element is overbroad because, by its plain meaning, it extends criminal consequences to "speech and expression" (or even nonexpressive conduct) "far removed from violence," Defs.' Br. at 10. In the defendants' view, that means the statute fails to bear an adequate relation between speech and violence under *Brandenburg*, which requires lawlessness to be the *likely* and *imminent* result of speech and expression.

Appearing to agree that a straightforward reading of this element to require only "a step toward" one of the purposes set forth under §2101(a)(1)-(4) would pose overbreadth problems, the government urges us to take after our sister circuit by construing it to require the actual "fulfillment" of one or more of these purposes. *Cf. Dellinger*, 472 F.2d at 361-62 ("assuming" such a view). So construed, the government contends that the statute necessitates "an adequate relation between . . . speech and action." *See id.*

We disagree with the parties. In our view, the presence of an overt-act element (or two, in fact), together with specific intent to incite or engage in a riot, simply indicates that the Anti-Riot Act was drafted as an *attempt* offense, of which it bears all the classic hallmarks, rather than a commission offense. *See Martin v. Taylor*, 857 F.2d 958, 961 (4th Cir. 1988) ("An attempt crime requires specific intent to commit a crime and some overt act which tends toward but falls short of the consummation of the crime."); *United States v. McFadden*, 739 F.2d 149, 152 (4th Cir. 1984) ("The classical elements of an attempt are intent to commit a crime, the execution of an overt act in furtherance of the intention, and a failure to consummate the crime."). Indeed, as the indictment in this very case illustrates, the crime described by §2101(a) is simply that of "Travel with Intent to Riot." . . .

Recall that an inchoate offense requires proof beyond a reasonable doubt that a defendant "intend[ed] to further an endeavor which, if completed, would satisfy all of the elements of a substantive criminal offense." *See Salinas [v. United States*, 522 U.S. 52 (1997),] at 65. Accordingly, to obtain a conviction under the Anti-Riot Act, the government must at a minimum prove that, notwithstanding any failure of consummation, the defendant acted with specific intent to engage in unprotected speech or conduct under §2101(a)(1)-(4). It's therefore with respect to the defendant's *intended* speech, as opposed to *actual* speech (if any), that *Brandenburg* mandates the adequate relation between words and lawless action for purposes of the Anti-Riot Act.

So framed, the central overbreadth question becomes whether any of the purposes included in the statute's specific-intent element implicate protected advocacy. If so, those purposes can't form the basis of an attempt to engage in unlawful speech, rendering overbroad the particular way of violating the statute described thereby.

We proceed to take up this question.

2.

The defendants contend that the specific-intent element is overbroad in two ways: (1) with respect to the plain meaning of the string of speech-related verbs under §2101(a)(2); and (2) with respect to the additional meaning that many of the speech-related verbs under §2101(a)(1)-(4) obtain under §2102(b). We take up each provision in turn.

i.

Because the First Amendment protects speech (the sine qua non of expression) as opposed to mere conduct, and because the purposes set forth under §2101(a)(1)-(4) encompass both speech- and mere conduct-related varieties, it's necessary to distinguish between them. Here, we agree with the parties, as well as our sister circuit, that the purposes implicating speech are those embodied by the verbs "incite," "organize," "promote," and "encourage" under §2101(a)(1)-(2). *See Dellinger*, 472 F.2d at 361.

With respect to "incite" under §2101(a)(1), we have little difficulty concluding that this verb encompasses no more than unprotected speech under *Brandenburg*. Thus, in the world of *Brandenburg*, "incite" most sensibly refers to speech that is directed and likely to produce an imminent lawlessness. The other conceivable definition is the dictionary one, which, as noted, is even narrower than *Brandenburg*'s because it requires lawlessness to occur, not just be likely. So either way, §2101(a)(1) readily comports with the First Amendment.

Turning to §2101(a)(2), however, we find that two verbs in the string "to organize, promote, [or] encourage" a riot fail to bear the requisite relation between speech and lawlessness. The loosest such relation in the bunch belongs to "encourage," which means simply "to attempt to persuade (someone) to do something." *See Encourage*, Merriam-Webster Unabridged, https://unabridged.merriamwebster.com/unabridged/encourage (last accessed July 30, 2020). Speech tending to encourage a riot thus encompasses *all* hypothetical efforts to advocate for a riot, including the vast majority that aren't *likely* to produce an *imminent* riot (even assuming they're *directed* to producing a riot). Indeed, because mere encouragement is quintessential protected advocacy, the Supreme Court has recognized that "[t]he mere tendency of speech to encourage unlawful acts is not a sufficient reason for banning it" under *Brandenburg. Ashcroft v. Free Speech Coalition*, 535 U.S. 234, 253 (2002); *see also Williams*, 553 U.S. at 300 (offering the statement, "I encourage you to obtain child pornography," as protected advocacy). It follows that *Brandenburg* protects speech having a mere tendency to encourage others to riot.

The verb "promote" occupies a similarly overinclusive position on the continuum of relation between advocacy and action. While "promote" admits of a wide range of meanings depending on context, we think that, in the context of an enterprise like a riot, it's best understood to mean "to support or encourage something," or "to advance" or "further something by helping to . . . introduce it." *See Promote*, Encarta Webster's Dictionary of the English Language (2d ed. 2004); *see also Promoter*, Encarta Webster's Dictionary of the English Language (2d ed. 2004) ("a supporter or advocate of something"); *cf. Williams*, 553 U.S. at 294 (defining "promote" to refer to "the act of recommending"). These definitions indicate that "promote" refers to a comparable, and perhaps even wider, range of riot-oriented advocacy as "encourage" in the context of §2101(a)(2). It thus suffers from the same overbreadth, subsuming an abundance of hypothetical efforts to persuade that aren't likely to produce an imminent riot. As a result, *Brandenburg* also protects speech having a mere tendency to promote others to riot. . . .

We . . . reject the government's invitation to limit both "promote" and "encourage" to advocacy that is directed and likely to produce an imminent riot. For starters, we don't think either verb is "readily susceptible" of such an artificial limitation. *See Stevens*, 559 U.S. at 481 (cleaned up). Moreover, because advocacy that is direct and likely to produce imminent lawlessness is already called "incitement," the government's proposed course would effectively require us to read these verbs as if they each said "incite" — the same term already found under §2101(a)(1). That, however, "requires rewriting, not just reinterpretation," and we may not "rewrite a law to conform it to constitutional requirements." *See Stevens*, 559 U.S. at 481 (cleaned up).

With respect to the verb "organize," however, we reach a different outcome. As it pertains to an event like a riot, "organize" is readily understood to mean "to form or establish something . . . by . . . bringing people together into a structured group," "to oversee the coordination of the various aspects of something" or "to arrange the components of something in a way that creates a particular structure." *See Organize*, Encarta Webster's Dictionary of the English Language (2d ed. 2004). We think speech tending to organize a riot might thus include communicating with prospective participants about logistics, arranging travel accommodations, or overseeing efforts to obtain weapons needed to carry out the planned violence.

Yet as these definitions and examples indicate, speech tending to "organize" others to riot consists *not* of mere abstract advocacy, but rather of concrete aid. For, by the time speech reaches the point of organizing a riot, it has crossed the line dividing abstract idea from material reality, even if its components must still be brought together, coordinated, arranged, or otherwise structured into form.

In other words, speech tending to organize a riot serves not to persuade others to engage in a hypothetical riot, but rather to facilitate the occurrence of a riot that has already begun to take shape. Such speech comes much closer to "preparing a group for violent action" than merely "teaching . . . the moral propriety" of violence in the abstract, *Brandenburg*, 395 U.S. at 48, and may even be characterized as the sort of "aiding and abetting of criminal conduct" that doesn't qualify for First Amendment protection, *see Rice*, 128 F.3d at 242-43. It follows that speech tending to organize a riot under §2101(a)(2), unlike that of encouraging and promoting a riot, doesn't implicate mere advocacy of lawlessness, and may thus be proscribed without reference to *Brandenburg*.

ii.

Turning to §2102(b), the defendants argue that this provision, which provides an admittedly curious gloss on the statute's specific-intent element, is overbroad in two ways. Since these arguments track the provision's two clauses, we take each in turn.

The first clause of §2102(b) provides that the term[ ] "'to incite a riot', or 'to organize, promote, encourage, participate in, or carry on a riot', includes, but is not limited to, urging or instigating other persons to riot." 18 U.S.C. §2102(b). Like the parties, we understand this clause to gloss two more purposes onto each subparagraph under §2101(a)(1)-(4) (excepting §2101(a)(3), "to commit any act of violence in furtherance of a riot"). These additional purposes are "urging" and "instigating" other persons to riot.

With respect to speech "instigating" others to riot, we agree with the parties this verb is best understood as a direct synonym for the dictionary definition of "incite" — which, as noted, is even narrower than *Brandenburg*'s. *See Instigate*, Encarta Webster's Dictionary of the English Language (2d ed. 2004) ("to cause a process to start"); *see also Instigate*, Merriam-Webster Unabridged, https://unabridged.merriam-webster.com/unabridged/instigate (last accessed July 30, 2020) ("provoke, incite"). In consequence, just as speech "instigating" others to riot seems to be already accounted for under §2101(a)(1), so too is it consistent with the First Amendment.

As to speech "urging" others to riot, however, we agree with the defendants that this verb suffers from a similarly inadequate relation between speech and lawless action as "encourage" and "promote" under §2101(a)(2). After all, to "urge" means simply to "encourage," "advocate," "recommend," or "advise . . . earnestly and with persistence." *Urge*, Encarta Webster's Dictionary of the English Language (2d ed. 2004); *see also Urge*, Merriam-Webster Unabridged, https://unabridged.merriamwebster.com/unabridged/urge (last accessed July 30, 2020) ("to present in an earnest and pressing manner" or "advocate or demand with importunity"). And because earnestness and persistence don't suffice to transform such forms of protected advocacy into speech that is likely to produce imminent lawless action, *Brandenburg* renders the purpose of "urging" others to riot overbroad.

The second clause of §2102(b) provides that the term[ ] "'to incite a riot', or 'to organize, promote, encourage, participate in, or carry on a riot' . . . shall not be deemed to mean the mere oral or written (1) advocacy of ideas or (2) expression of belief, not involving advocacy of any act or acts of violence or assertion of the rightness of, or the right to commit, any such act or acts." 18 U.S.C. §2102(b). Phrased in simpler terms, this clause provides that each of these purposes under §2101(a) shall *not* be deemed to encompass the mere advocacy of ideas or beliefs *not* involving advocacy of violence.

The defendants argue that the last phrase of this clause, beginning with "not involving," is overbroad. They point out that "mere advocacy of the use of force or violence does not remove speech from the protection of the First Amendment" in a *Brandenburg* world. *See NAACP v. Claiborne Hardware Co.*, 458 U.S. 886, 927 (1982) (emphasis omitted). And they contend that, owing to the double-negative construction of the second clause of §2102(b), the final phrase must be construed as affirmatively criminalizing mere advocacy of violence, running afoul of its protected status. . . .

. . . [B]ecause Congress drafted the Anti-Riot Act against the backdrop of a long line of cases . . . in which mere advocacy of violence was regularly held to be unprotected, we find it all the more likely that the exclusion found in the final phrase of §2102(b) means to attach criminal consequences to such advocacy, and isn't just indifferent to it. We therefore hold this language to be overbroad as well.

3.

The defendants' final overbreadth argument concerns the Anti-Riot Act's definition of a "riot" under §2102(a). They contend that this definition is overbroad because it contains the clear-and-present-danger test that *Brandenburg* displaced from the prevailing incitement test. The government responds that, while the clear-and-present-danger test is no longer part of the prevailing incitement test, it's nonetheless flexible enough that we may construe it consistently with *Brandenburg*'s tightened standard. . . .

To revisit §2102(a), that provision defines two types of riot: the first based on one or more "acts of violence," 18 U.S.C. §2102(a)(1), and the second based on one or more "threats" to commit one or more acts of violence, *id.* §2102(a)(2). With respect to each type, the clear-and-present-danger test governs only the relation between the act or threat of violence forming the core of the riotous conduct and the resulting risk of "damage or injury" to the "property" or "person" of any other individual. *See id.* §2102(a). So, whatever the precise measure of risk required by that test, a "riot" entails at bottom an act or a threat of violence presenting "grave danger" to others. *Cf. United States v. Matthews*, 419 F.2d 1177, 1180-82, 1184 (D.C. Cir. 1969) (discussing the District of Columbia's anti-riot statute, passed by Congress in late 1967, which defines a "riot" similarly to §2102(a) as a public disturbance "which by tumultuous and violent conduct or the threat thereof creates grave danger of damage or injury to property or persons").

We think it plain that both types of riot describe conduct that Congress had the right to prevent in enacting the Anti-Riot Act. Indeed, regardless of any risk of bodily injury or property damage, acts of violence against others in and of themselves constitute well-recognized forms of unlawful conduct, finding no protection under the first or any other amendment. As for "threats of violence," they too "are outside the First Amendment" under the doctrine of true threats, which "protects individuals" from even "the possibility that the threatened violence will occur." *R.A.V. v. City of St. Paul*, 505 U.S. 377, 388 (1992); *see also Virginia v. Black*, 538 U.S. 343, 359-60 (2003) (plurality opinion) (discussing "true threats"). And we have little trouble reading "threat" under §2102(a) to contemplate only such true threats, which are frequently made unlawful as well.

Thus, like our sister circuit, we conclude that Congress in §2102(a) has managed to describe "a disorder of a type which is enough of an assault on the property and personal safety interests of the community" that inciting, engaging in, or aiding and abetting one "can be made a criminal offense." *See Dellinger*, 472 F.2d at 360-61. Accordingly, we discern no overbreadth in the statute's definition of a riot.

D.

Having found that the Anti-Riot Act is overbroad vis-à-vis *Brandenburg* insofar as it proscribes speech tending to "encourage" or "promote" a riot, as well as speech "urging" others to riot or "involving" mere advocacy of violence, we turn now to consider whether the amount of overbreadth is substantial, "not only in an absolute sense, but also relative to the statute's plainly legitimate sweep." *Williams*, 553 U.S. at 292. We conclude that it is.

To be sure, the Anti-Riot Act has a plainly legitimate sweep. The statute validly proscribes not only efforts to engage in such unprotected speech as inciting, instigating, and organizing a riot, but also such unprotected conduct as participating in, carrying on, and committing acts of violence in furtherance of a riot, as well as aiding and abetting any person engaged in such conduct. In other words, it encompasses just about every form of unprotected activity in relation to a riot. And the statute's conduct-related applications appear to form the basis of every reported prosecution under it.

Yet the Anti-Riot Act nonetheless sweeps up a substantial amount of protected advocacy. Whereas *Brandenburg* removes advocacy relating to a riot from the protection of the First Amendment only if it is directed and likely to produce an imminent riot, the statute purports to regulate any speech tending merely to "encourage," "promote," or "urge" others to riot, as well as mere advocacy of any act of violence. Altogether, these areas of overbreadth cover the whole realm of advocacy that *Brandenburg* protects, and dwarfs that which it left unprotected. Thus, while the statute may have been perfectly consistent with the contemporary understanding of the First Amendment when it was enacted, *Brandenburg* causes it to encroach substantially upon free speech.

E.

Having concluded that the Anti-Riot Act is substantially overbroad in part, we turn at last to consider whether the overbroad portions of the statute are severable from the constitutionally valid remainder; if so, only those portions are "to be invalidated." *See Ferber*, 458 U.S. at 769 n.24. We agree with the government that they are.

Because facial invalidation "is strong medicine" that serves "as a last resort," *id.* at 769, the "normal rule" in the case of a partially unconstitutional statute is "that partial, rather than facial, invalidation is the required course," *Free Enter. Fund. v. Pub. Co. Accounting Oversight Bd.*, 561 U.S. 477, 508 (2010) (cleaned up). Indeed, the Supreme Court has repeatedly cautioned that "whenever an act of Congress contains unobjectionable provisions separable from those found to be unconstitutional," it is our "duty" as a court to "maintain the act in so far as it is valid." *Regan v. Time, Inc.*, 468 U.S. 641, 652 (1984) (plurality opinion) (cleaned up); *see also Seila Law LLC v. Consumer Fin. Prot. Bureau*, 140 S. Ct. 2183, 2209 (2020) (plurality opinion) ("Generally speaking, when confronting a constitutional flaw in a statute, we try to limit the solution to the problem, severing any problematic portions while leaving the remainder intact." (cleaned up)). . . .

Thus, "[e]ven in the absence of a severability clause, the traditional rule is that the unconstitutional provision must be severed unless the statute created in its absence is legislation that Congress would not have enacted." *Seila Law*, 140 S. Ct. at 2209 (cleaned up). Put differently, "we must retain those portions of the [a]ct that are (1) constitutionally valid, (2) capable of functioning independently, and (3) consistent with Congress' basic objectives in enacting the statute." *United States v. Booker*, 543 U.S. 220, 259 (2005) (cleaned up); *see also Seila Law*, 140 S. Ct. at 2209. . . .

Applying these principles to the Anti-Riot Act, we hold that the appropriate remedy is to invalidate no more than the language responsible for the statute's overbreadth. That language consists of the words "encourage," "promote," and "urging" under §§2101(a)(2) and 2102(b), as well as the final phrase of §2102(b), beginning with the words "not involving" and continuing through the end of that provision. Severed accordingly, these provisions of the statute look like this:

(a) Whoever travels in interstate or foreign commerce or uses any facility of interstate or foreign commerce, including, but not limited to, the mail, telegraph, telephone, radio, or television, with intent — . . .

> (2) to organize, ~~promote, encourage,~~ participate in, or carry on a riot;

. . .

and who either during the course of any such travel or use or thereafter performs or attempts to perform any other overt act for any purpose specified in subparagraph (A), (B), (C), or (D) of this paragraph[] —

Shall be fined under this title, or imprisoned not more than five years, or both.

18 U.S.C. §2101(a)(2).

> As used in this chapter, the term "to incite a riot", or "to organize, ~~promote, encourage,~~ participate in, or carry on a riot", includes, but is not limited to, ~~urging or~~ instigating other persons to riot, but shall not be deemed to mean the mere oral or written (1) advocacy of ideas or (2) expression of belief, ~~not involving advocacy of any act or acts of violence or assertion of the rightness of, or the right to commit, any such act or acts.~~

Id. §2102(b).

Besides these discrete instances of overbreadth, the remainder of the Anti-Riot Act "is perfectly valid." *See Booker*, 543 U.S. at 258. It's also capable of functioning independently and thus "fully operative without the offending" language. *See Seila Law*, 140 S. Ct. at 2209. After all, that language makes up only a fraction of the statute's specific-intent element, consisting of just two items from a menu of alternative purposes under §2101(a)(1)-(4), plus two additional purposes glossed onto these by way of §2102(b). . . .

Further, such minimal severance is consistent with Congress's basic objective in enacting the Anti-Riot Act. We think that objective is to proscribe, to the maximum permissible extent, unprotected speech and conduct that both relates to a riot and involves the use of interstate commerce. And while Congress drafted the statute to encompass the full scope of such unprotected speech as of 1968, our partial invalidation serves only to remove the discrete purposes that *Brandenburg* rendered overbroad, thereby trimming the statute's scope without altering its meaning. We thus have no doubt that, if Congress could have foreseen the Court's decision in *Brandenburg*, it would have readily preferred to enact this appropriately narrowed version of the statute [rather] than none at all. . . .

IV.

As an alternative ground for facial invalidation, the defendants contend that the Anti-Riot Act is void for vagueness under the Due Process Clause of the Fifth Amendment. We disagree. . . .

The defendants argue that the Anti-Riot Act is unduly vague primarily with respect to its definition of a riot under §2102(a). Not so. In our view, the definition provides more than the "minimal guidelines" necessary to provide a sufficient standard of conduct and enforcement for purposes of due process. *See Kolender* [*v. Lawson*, 461 U.S. 352, 358 (1983)].

Recall that §2102(a) describes two types of "riot": one based on actual violence and another based on a threat of violence. *See* 18 U.S.C. §2102(a). Each type breaks down into roughly four elements. An actual-violence riot consists of (1) a "public disturbance," (2) involving one or more "acts of violence," (3) committed "by one or more persons" who form part of a group "of three or more persons," and (4) that either "result[s] in[ ] damage or injury to the property . . . or . . . person of any other individual" or "constitute[s] a clear and present danger" of such damage or injury. *See id.* §2102(a)(1). Similarly, a threat-of-violence riot consists of (1) a "public disturbance," (2) involving one or more "threats" to commit an act of violence, (3) committed "by one or more persons" who form part of a group of "three or more persons" and have "the ability of immediate execution" of the threat or threats, and (4) that, if executed, would either result in "damage or injury to the property . . . or . . . person of any other individual" or constitute a clear and present danger of such damage or injury. *See id.* §2102(a)(2). . . .

In particular, §2102(a)'s requirement that the public disturbance involve either an act or threat of *violence* renders the scope of proscribed conduct significantly more definite. Indeed, because the word "violence" has a settled and objective meaning, the definition's violence element serves to exclude a wide range of conduct that might constitute a "public disturbance" judged subjectively — such as "making an unnecessary or distracting noise," *see Breach of the Peace*, Black's Law Dictionary (10th ed. 2014); or, as the defendants hypothesize, causing a "public uproar" on Twitter, *see* Defs.' Br. at 31 n.5.

In fact, because *any* act or threat of violence inherently constitutes a disturbance or breach of the peace, the definition's public-disturbance element appears in context to mean simply that the act or threat of violence must occur in a public setting — as, for instance, with each of the three rallies at which the defendants conducted *their* acts of violence.

So construed, the core elements of §2102(a) leave little to the imagination.

The statute's definition of a riot is further narrowed by §2102(a)'s remaining elements. Under the third, the act or threat of violence constituting the public disturbance must be committed by someone who forms part of a group of at least three people, thereby ensuring that more ordinary instances of violence, accomplished by less than a crowd of three, don't rise to the level of riotous conduct. Under the fourth, the act or threat of violence must either cause bodily injury or property damage or create a clear and present danger of the same, thereby excluding violence that entails an insignificant or remote risk of harm to others. . . .

V. . . .

Before accepting the defendants' guilty pleas, the district court was required to "determine that there [was] a factual basis" for them, Fed. R. Crim. P. 11(b)(3), which it did by accepting the defendants' respective Statements of Offense. In those Statements, the defendants stipulated that the substantive offense conduct underlying their respective conspiracy convictions consists (beyond such overt acts as traveling to rallies through interstate commerce, conducting combat training, and buying supplies) of engaging "in violent confrontations," J.A. 227, which is to say "physical conflict," J.A. 232, with counterprotestors at each of the three rallies discussed above. Specifically, the defendants admitted to having each (as part of an assemblage of three or more) "personally committed multiple violent acts" — including but not limited to pushing, punching, kicking, choking, head-butting, and otherwise assaulting numerous individuals, and none of which "were in self-defense" — in Huntington Beach, Berkeley, and Charlottesville. J.A. 231, 236.

Such substantive offense conduct qualifies manifestly as "commit[ting] any act of violence in furtherance of a riot" within the ordinary meaning of §2101(a)(3), as well "participat[ing] in" and "carry[ing] on a riot" within the ordinary meaning of §2101(a)(2) — three wholly conduct-oriented purposes left unscathed by our partial invalidation of the statute. By the same token, the defendants' offenses have manifestly nothing to do with speech tending to encourage, promote, or urge others to riot; mere advocacy of violence; or any other First Amendment activity; as the district court properly found. *See* [*United States v. Daley*, 378 F. Supp. 3d 539, 559 (W.D. Va. 2019)] (noting that the First Amendment doesn't "immunize[ ] violence," even "within the broader context of a political demonstration"). The defendants muster no argument to the contrary.

Moreover, as noted, the defendants have necessarily conceded — consistent with the "usual judicial practice" in overbreadth cases, *see* [*Bd. of Trustees of State Univ. of N.Y. v. Fox*, 492 U.S. 469, 484-85 (1989)]; *Preston*, 660 F.3d at 737-38 — that the Anti-Riot Act poses no constitutional concern as applied to their own conduct. And indeed, *none* of the defendants' overbreadth theories, including those we have rejected, provide any basis for an as-applied challenge on the facts to which they have stipulated. It follows that anything less than facial invalidation of the statute affords the defendants no relief from their convictions. *Cf. Regan*, 468 U.S. at 659 (holding that 18 U.S.C. §504 as partially invalidated wasn't unconstitutional "as applied" to the challenger, whose offense conduct qualified under "the remaining portions of the statute").

* * *

For the foregoing reasons, the judgments of the district court are

Affirmed.

[NSL p. 1048, CTL p. 700. Insert at end of Note 2.]

One commentator explained the outcome in *Stone* in this way:

[T]he group's amateurism and disorganization made it an awkward fit for the charges. Peter Henning, a professor at Wayne State University School of Law in neighboring Detroit, cautioned after the trial that militia groups shouldn't "read[] too much into" the acquittal. The Hutaree were "almost a gang that couldn't shoot straight." [Judge] Roberts notes, for example, that the Hutaree chat about cop murder but "never come to a consensus or agreement on ways in which to oppose federal agents by force." Their disorganization and lack of planning made the high standards for "conspiracy" a bad match. [Jacob Schulz, *The Last Time the Justice Department Prosecuted a Seditious Conspiracy Case*, Lawfare, Feb. 24, 2021.]

Tragically, no one could say that Sheik Rahman's group "couldn't shoot straight."

This distinction might also apply to seditious conspiracy charges against some of the participants in the January 6, 2021 U.S. Capitol riots. Their conspiracy, if proven, was accompanied by violence that had not yet occurred in the *Stone* conspiracy. "Storming the Capitol and trying to track them down sure seems like 'an exertion of force.'" *Id.*

[NSL p. 1156, CTL p. 808. Insert after Note 6.]

6a. A Torture Test Case? Notwithstanding the constraints identified above, the military judge presiding over the *USS Cole* trial ruled in May 2021 that the government *could* use statements a defendant made while being tortured in CIA custody — not against him at trial, but in support of pre-trial motions. *See United States v. Al Nashiri*, No. AE353AA (Mil. Comm'n May 18, 2021). As Judge Acosta explained, the MCA only governs when coerced statements are "admissible in a military commission," which he viewed as a reference to the *trial* itself, and not to pre-trial proceedings even in the same case. Does that seem like a fair reading of the statutory text? Of Congress's intent? Al Nashiri has sought review of that decision in the Court of Military Commission Review via a petition for a writ of mandamus.

According to news reports, a dispute within the Biden administration over the government's position on appeal led to the resignation of General Mark Martins, who had served as the commissions' Chief Prosecutor for more than a decade. *See* Carol Rosenberg, *Chief Guantánamo Prosecutor Resigning Before Sept. 11 Trial Begins*, N.Y. Times, July 9, 2021. If Al Nashiri is unable to satisfy the very high bar for mandamus relief, does leaving such a pre-trial ruling intact increase the possibility that any conviction would be reversed on post-conviction appeal? If so, and if the coerced statements aren't central to the government's case-in-chief, why do you suppose the government insisted on pursuing their admission?

[NSL p. 1164, CTL p. 816. Insert before Notes and Questions.]

The manuscript for this edition of the casebook was completed before the emergence of the COVID-19 pandemic in early 2020. But we might have learned from the TOPOFF exercise 20 years earlier that a biological threat to national security could arise from natural causes as well as from a terrorist attack, and that such a threat would present many of the same challenges.

Hardly anyone doubts that COVID-19 posed such a threat. *See, e.g.,* Lisa Monaco, *Pandemic Disease Is a Threat to National Security*, Foreign Aff., Mar. 3, 2020. When it arrived, it brought death to more than 600,000 Americans (as of this writing in June 2021), more than died in combat in all the wars of the twentieth century, and catastrophic damage to the U.S. economy. President Trump described himself as a "wartime president" fighting an "invisible enemy." Caitlin Oprysko & Susannah Luthi, *Trump Labels Himself "A Wartime President" Combating Coronavirus*, Politico, Mar. 18, 2020. Some argue that these losses resulted, at least in part, from inadequate planning and failed leadership. Others say the effects of the pandemic might have been greatly reduced if existing laws and plans had been effectively implemented.

Among the critical questions that need answers at this point are (1) how existing laws and plans might be improved to respond more effectively to the next pandemic — because COVID-19 is surely not the final one; (2) how to ensure that the government makes full use of its existing powers to protect the American people; (3) how to assign responsibilities for responding among federal, state, and tribal governments; and (4) how to balance the regulation of individuals and businesses during a pandemic against affected liberty interests.

An extensive chronology of developments during the pandemic, with links to sources, may be found at Ryan Goodman & Danielle Schulkin, *Timeline of the Coronavirus Pandemic and U.S. Response*, Just Security, Nov. 3, 2020. Many key legal issues are analyzed in *Law and the COVID-19 Pandemic*, 11 J. Nat'l Security L. & Pol'y 1-197 (2020); *COVID-19: The Legal Challenges* (Stephen Dycus & Eugene R. Fidell, eds. 2021).

[NSL p. 1166, CTL p. 818. Insert at the end of Note 3.]

Communication and public outreach are vital components of effective pandemic preparedness and response. Government officials must provide clear, accurate information and guidance about the health risk and suggested mitigation measures that will allow the American public to help protect their own health and the health of others.

For months after the COVID-19 virus began to spread in the United States in 2020, however, President Trump sought to reassure the American public that the risks were minimal, comparing the coronavirus to the common flu, and claiming that the disease was "totally under control." Glenn Kessler, Meg Kelly & Sarah Cahlan, *Tracking Trump's False or Misleading Coronavirus Claims*, Wash. Post, Mar. 14, 2020. He offered these assurances even as he received urgent warnings from intelligence and public health officials about the looming danger. *See*

Eric Lipton et al., *He Could Have Seen What Was Coming: Behind Trump's Failure on the Virus*, N.Y. Times, updated Oct. 2, 2020. Privately, however, he maintained that he deliberately minimized the threat because he didn't want to "create a panic." *Trump Tells Woodward He Deliberately Downplayed Coronavirus Threat*, NPR, Sept. 10, 2020. According to some critics, he was motivated chiefly by concerns that bad news might hurt the economy and his chances for reelection in November. Reports that the White House ordered the CDC to moderate its advice to the public about protective measures seem to confirm this criticism. *See, e.g.*, Amy Goldstein & Lena H. Sun, *Controversial Change in Guidelines about Coronavirus Testing Directed by the White House Coronavirus Task Force*, Wash. Post, Aug. 26, 2020.

Efforts by media to obtain and disseminate accurate information about the pandemic were frustrated by legislation or executive actions in a number of states that altered rules for access to public records, and by federal agencies' refusal or delay in responding to FOIA requests. *See* Adam A. Marshall & Gunita Singh, *Access to Public Records and the Role of the News Media in Providing Information about COVID19*, 11 J. Nat'l Security L. & Pol'y 199 (2020). They were further hampered by restricted reporting of data by the CDC on orders from political appointees. Sheryl Gay Stolberg, *Trump Administration Strips C.D.C. of Control of Coronavirus Data*, N.Y. Times, July 14, 2020; Dan Diamond, *Trump Officials Interfered with CDC Reports on Covid-19*, Politico, Sept. 11, 2020.

Can you say how government information might influence public behavior that could, in turn, affect efforts to contain and mitigate the pandemic? Whether or not you believe that information from the media about a great emergency should sometimes be regulated, do you think the government should disseminate all information available to it about an emergeency? Can you think of ways to avoid official pronouncements that are politically motivated?

Should government messaging always be true? Suppose the truth might cause a panic — such as a run on stores or even a chaotic flight from an infected area? In March 2020, the U.S. Surgeon General tweeted that people should stop buying masks, and Dr. Anthony Fauci testified that the public did not need them, reportedly out of concern that the United States was running out of supplies for health care workers. *See* Megan Molteni & Adam Rogers, *How Masks Went From Don't-Wear to Must-Have*, Wired, Jul. July 2, 2020. Should they have been more truthful about the utility of masks, since widely seen as a key safeguard against the spread of COVID-19?

[NSL p. 1170, CTL p. 822. Insert before Notes and Questions.]

4. Planning for a Pandemic

A dizzying array of federal statutes, regulations, and other authorities are particularly relevant to planning for infectious disease pandemics, whether they are naturally occurring or manufactured. Some of these rules — like the multitude of plans they authorize — overlap, many are redundant or ambiguous, and others conflict. They also clearly fail to address some predictable developments. Together they leave unresolved important questions about responsibility, accountability, and constitutionality.

The Pandemic and All-Hazards Preparedness Act, Pub. L. No. 109-417, 120 Stat. 2831 (2006), for example, seeks to integrate the DHS into a public health system based largely on state authorities and a mostly private healthcare system. The act provides that the HHS Secretary will "lead all Federal public health and medical response to public health emergencies and incidents covered by the National Response Plan." *Id.* §101(2), 42 U.S.C. §300hh(a). It also calls for preparation of a quadrennial National Health Security Strategy, consistent with the NIMS and the National Response Plan, that includes monitoring of diseases at home and abroad; containment, including isolation, quarantine, and social distancing; risk communication and public preparedness; and rapid distribution of medical countermeasures. *Id.* §103, 42 U.S.C. §300hh-1. *See* Sarah A. Lister & Frank Gottron, *The Pandemic and All-Hazards Preparedness Act (P.L. 109-417): Provisions and Changes to Preexisting Law* (Cong. Res. Serv. RL33589), Mar. 12, 2007.

In 2015 the Obama administration established a new Global Health Security and Biodefense unit within the National Security Council. Its job was to monitor global health risks and to provide expertise and recommendations to key decision makers in the event of a global health crisis. But the unit's leader was dismissed, and its functions were folded into a new directorate focused on counterproliferation and biodefense in a reorganization of the NSC by John Bolton in 2018. *See* Glenn Kessler & Meg Kelly, *Was the White House Office for Global Pandemics Eliminated?*, Wash. Post, Mar. 20, 2020; Kimberly Dozier & Vera Bergengruen, *Under Fire For Coronavirus Response, Trump Officials Defend Disbanding Pandemic Team*, Life, Mar. 19, 2020.

The National Defense Authorization Act for Fiscal Year 2017, Pub. L. No. 114-328, §1086, 130 Stat. 2000, 2423 (2016) (codified at 6 U.S.C. §104), required DOD, HHS, DHS, and USDA to jointly develop a national biodefense strategy and implementation plan. And the Pandemic and All-Hazards Preparedness and Advancing Innovation Act, Pub. L. No. 116-22 (2019), called for identification of threats and response plans, and an annual review of the Strategic National Stockpile to ensure against its depletion.

Drawing on these statutory authorities, a 2018 *National Biodefense Strategy* and National Security Presidential Memorandum-14 (NSPM-14), *Presidential Memorandum on the Support for National Biodefense* (Sept. 18, 2018), directed the creation of a governance structure to coordinate responses of relevant federal agencies. GAO, however, found no "clearly documented methods, guidance, processes, and roles and responsibilities for enterprise-wide decision-making." Gov't Accountability Off., *National Biodefense Strategy: Additional Efforts Would Enhance Likelihood of Effective Implementation* (GAO20-273) 2 (Feb. 2020).

In January 2019, HHS published its *National Health Security Strategy 2019-2022*, outlining a "whole-of-government" federal plan to support state, local, tribal, and territorial authorities in a public health emergency. The *Strategy* stressed the need for early detection of potential pandemic infectious diseases, and for making available safe, effective countermeasures, including vaccines. And it called for creation of a "resilient medical supply chain."

An additional plan to respond specifically to COVID-19 was published in 2020, after the pandemic was well underway. Dep't of Health & Human Servs., *PanCAP Adapted U.S. Gov't Covid-19 Response Plan* (Mar. 13, 2020). Filled with broad bureaucratic jargon and marked "not for public distribution or release," it outlined federal actions pursuant to the *National Response Framework* and the *Biological Incident Annex to the Response and Recovery Federal Interagency Operational Plans* (Jan. 2017). According to this plan, the CDC established a COVID-19 Incident Management System on January 7, 2020, while FEMA activated several Emergency Support Functions to assist HHS. The plan pledged to provide "accurate, coordinated, and timely information to affected audiences," and to "stabilize medical supply chains," *PanCAP, supra*, at 29, 42, although neither of these goals was subsequently met. It did, however, fulfil its promise to develop an effective vaccine. Notably, the March 2020 plan called for no mandatory regulations for businesses or individuals, aside from screening and temporary quarantines for some international travelers.

At the beginning of his administration, President Biden ordered his National Security Adviser to take charge of biodefense preparedness, notwithstanding contrary provisions of NSPM-14, and he directed a newly created COVID-19 Response Coordinator to manage the federal response to the ongoing pandemic. Exec. Order No. 13,987, *Organizing and Mobilizing the United States Government to Provide a Unified and Effective Response to Combat COVID-19 and to Provide United States Leadership on Global Health and Security*, §3(c), 86 Fed. Reg. 7019 (Jan. 20, 2021).

5. The Domestic Terrorism Threat

The threat of terrorism emanating from domestic sources is not new. From the Ku Klux Klan's post-Reconstruction campaign of terror to intimidate Black voters and their supporters, to the 1995 bombing of the Alfred P. Murrah Federal Building in Oklahoma by anti-government extremists that killed 168 people, to the January 6, 2021 incursion into the U.S. Capitol by groups and individuals seeking to disrupt the counting of the 2020 electoral votes, extremism has been part of the American experience across the years.

The threat has evolved, however. In a study ordered by President Biden on his first day in office, federal intelligence and law enforcement communities characterized the threat posed by domestic extremists as "elevated," with the two most lethal elements of that threat coming from (1) violent extremists who advocate for white supremacy and (2) anti-government or anti-authority violent extremists, such as militia movements. *See* Off. of the Dir. of Nat'l Intelligence, *Domestic Violent Extremism Poses Heightened Threat in 2021* (Mar. 1, 2021), https://www.dhs.gov/sites/default/files/publications/21_0301_odni_uncla ss-summary-of-dve-assessment-17_march-final_508.pdf.

The Biden administration has taken several steps to address this threat. The Department of Homeland Security for the first time identified domestic violent extremism as a policy priority and created a domestic terrorism branch within its Office of Intelligence and Analysis focused on monitoring social media for indications of eminent violence hiding "in plain sight." *See* Carly Gordenstein & Seamus Hughes, *A Sea Change in Counterterrorism*, Lawfare, June 16, 2021. DOJ, for its part, has requested additional funding for domestic terrorism investigations and prosecutions, and has centralized oversight of domestic violent extremism cases in the National Security Division. *Id.* In addition, the White House in June 2021 issued its first *National Strategy for Countering Domestic Terrorism*, https://www.whitehouse.gov/wp-content/uploads/2021/06/National-Strategy-for-Countering-Domestic-Terrorism.pdf. The document seeks to foster a government-wide strategy to counter domestic terrorists. It is organized around four "pillars": better information sharing, curtailing recruitment and mobilization to violence, disrupting and deterring domestic terrorism activity, and confronting long-term contributors to domestic terrorism. On a practical level, exactly what this framework will mean is unclear. Nevertheless, echoing recent measures undertaken at DHS, it calls for closer scrutiny of public social media posts as well as better information sharing and coordination among government agencies. Notably, the strategy does not call for a new criminal law focused on domestic terrorism as a substantive crime.

[NSL p. 1171, CTL p. 823. Insert at the end of Note 4.]

In fall 2020, President Trump said that he was "counting on the military" to deliver COVID-19 vaccines to the public. In fact, the military was not used for any deliveries or to administer shots. But the Pentagon still played a significant logistical role. *See* Jennifer Steinhauer, *Military's Role in Vaccine Will Be Strictly Behind the Scenes, Despite Trump's Claims*, N.Y. Times, Nov. 26, 2020.

[NSL p. 1171, CTL p. 823. Insert after the second paragraph of Note 5.]

As we learned in 2021, these cyber-based threats to the homeland do not originate solely with government actors. A series of high-profile — and highly disruptive — ransomware attacks launched by criminal syndicates believed to be based in Russia further illustrated the vulnerabilities of critical infrastructure stemming from inadequate cyber defenses. In one incident, Colonial Pipeline, owner of a pipeline that delivers 45% of the East Coast's fuel supplies, shut down 5,500 miles of pipeline as the result of a ransomware attack. The shutdown was not severe enough to create an actual fuel shortage, but a consumer run on gasoline led to long lines at service stations in the days following the shutdown. *See* David E. Sanger, Clifford Krauss & Nicole Perlroth, *Cyberattack Forces a Shutdown of a Top U.S. Pipeline*, N.Y. Times, May 8, 2021. Just weeks later, a similar attack on JBS, the world's largest meat supplier, forced a brief shutdown of nine beef plants in the United States and disrupted production at poultry and pork plants. *See* Julie Creswell, Nicole Perlroth & Noam Scheiber, *Ransomware Disrupts Meat Plants in Latest Attack on Critical U.S. Business*, N.Y. Times, June 1, 2021.

[NSL p. 1172, CTL 824. Insert after Note 5.]

5.1. A New "Greatest Threat" — COVID-19. A new grave threat to homeland security emerged in 2020 with the arrival of the COVID-19 pandemic. Compared to a regional or nationwide power blackout, this threat was relatively slow to develop. But its effects on the nation's population and the economy have been devastating, and it has created enormous stresses on government institutions — indeed, on democratic government itself.

Responses to the spreading contagion were mounted by various federal agencies, all apparently influenced to some degree by political concerns within the White House. HHS's Assistant Secretary for Preparedness and Response (ASPR) is the official statutorily designated to lead preparedness for and response to public health emergencies. 42 U.S.C. §300hh-10. In March 2020, however, the lead agency role was shifted from HHS to FEMA, which coordinated with a White House Task Force. *See* FEMA, *Pandemic Response to Coronavirus Disease 2019 (COVID-19): Initial Assessment Report* (Jan. 13, 2021). FEMA summed up preparations for the pandemic this way:

> Federal pandemic planning was insufficient for a national incident and did not account for interagency operations, resource shortages, and an integrated federal approach to supporting SLTT [state, local, tribal, and territorial] partners effectively. The [secret] 2018 Pandemic Crisis Action Plan (PanCAP) did not envision FEMA as the agency leading federal response for a whole-of-government response under the Stafford Act, or its role in managing health and medical supplies and equipment for SLTT partners nationally. FEMA regional pandemic plans either did not exist or did not account for jurisdiction-specific capabilities or deficiencies. [*Id.* at 11.]

FEMA also noted a "lack of clarity" about its authorities and roles. *Id.* at 8. For its part, DHS reported that it concerned itself in 2020 chiefly with associated risks from transnational criminal organizations and illegal immigration, malevolent cyber activities, foreign influence campaigns, disruption of medical equipment supply lines, and domestic violence spurred by mitigation efforts. Dep't of Homeland Security, *Homeland Threat Assessment* (Oct. 2020).

FEMA's self-evaluation contains a number of findings and recommendations to prepare for the next pandemic. *Pandemic Response to Coronavirus Disease, supra,* at 139-152. Can you guess, without looking, what they include?

Can you say why relevant statutes, regulations, and other protocols have not provided greater predictability and accountability during the COVID-19 crisis? How could the rules and plans be improved? What could be done to ensure their effective utilization in the next pandemic?

Momentum for a broader investigation into the COVID-19 pandemic is growing. Private foundations have initiated one ongoing inquiry, which, at this writing, "has already interviewed more than 200 public health experts, business leaders, elected officials, victims and their families," while bipartisan bills creating a COVID-19 commission have been introduced in both the House and the Senate. *See* Sheryl Gay Stolberg, *Calls Grow in the U.S. for a Commission to Investigate the Pandemic*, N.Y. Times. June 16, 2021.

[NSL p. 1178, CTL p. 830. Insert after Note 1.]

1.1. Lockdown: COVID-19 Restrictions. When the COVID-19 virus began spreading around the world in early 2020, a number of countries restricted international travel or simply closed their borders. Many imposed domestic controls, as well, closing schools and businesses, limiting the size of public gatherings, requiring the wearing of masks, and ordering citizens to remain in their homes except for medical care or purchase of "essential" supplies.

A number of U.S. states and cities also adopted at least some of these measures, which were described by public health authorities as critical to containment of the virus. But the restrictions were extremely unpopular with many Americans, who worried that they would cost jobs or jeopardize businesses, as indeed they have. Some also objected to the inconvenience of school closures, the educational cost and social inequity of moving fitfully to online instruction, and limits on travel. Others resisted social distancing and mask wearing because, they argued, they were not afraid of becoming ill — ignoring the fact that such precautions were intended primarily to protect others from infection. Some even insisted that the pandemic was a hoax.

a. Restrictions on International Travel

Like other nations around the world, the United States imposed curbs on entry by international travelers in response to the pandemic. At the end of January 2020, President Trump began issuing orders that barred entry from certain countries where coronavirus outbreaks had occurred, including China, Iran, many European states, the United Kingdom, and

Ireland. He also closed the borders with Mexico and Canada. *See* U.S. Dep't of State, Bur. of Consular Aff., *Presidential Proclamations on Novel Coronavirus* (updated Jan. 26, 2021). Each of the orders included numerous exceptions. Travelers arriving from certain areas were placed under a mandatory 14-day quarantine, others only if they showed symptoms of disease.

Each order was said to be authorized by the Immigration and Nationality Act, 8 U.S.C. §§1182(f), 1185(a), which allows the President to bar or restrict any aliens whose entry he finds would be "detrimental to the interests of the United States," or by the Public Health Service Act, 42 U.S.C. §265, which permits exclusion of persons from a country where a communicable disease exists.

The timing and efficacy of these orders were questioned by many. *See, e.g.*, Elizabeth Goitein, *Emergency Powers, Real and Imagined: How President Trump Used and Failed to Use Presidential Authority in the COVID-19 Crisis*, 11 J. Nat'l Security L. & Pol'y 27, 31-37 (2020); Thomas J. Bollyky & Jennifer B. Nuzzo, Opinion, *Trump's "Early" Travel "Bans" Weren't Early, Weren't Bans and Didn't Work*, Wash. Post, Oct. 1, 2020. They were nevertheless continued and expanded by President Biden. Proc. No. 10,143, *Suspension of Entry as Immigrants and Non-Immigrants of Certain Additional Persons Who Pose a Risk of Transmitting Coronavirus Disease*, 86 Fed. Reg. 7467 (Jan. 25, 2021).

President Trump also banned entry into the United States by all non-U.S. persons, again with many exceptions, ostensibly to protect American workers during the COVID-19 crisis. Proc. No. 10,014, *Suspending Entry of Immigrants Who Present Risk to the U.S. Labor Market During the Economic Recovery Following the COVID-19 Outbreak*, 85 Fed. Reg. 23,441 (Apr. 22, 2020). But some viewed the measure as part of an effort extending over several years to reduce all immigration. *See* Muzaffar Chishti & Sarah Pierce, *The U.S. Stands Alone in Explicitly Basing Coronavirus-Linked Immigration Restrictions on Economic Grounds*, Migration Pol'y Inst., May 29, 2020.

b. Federal Restrictions on Domestic Activities

On January 31, 2020, the HHS Secretary declared a public health emergency under the Public Health Service Act, 42 U.S.C. §247d(a), which authorizes the Secretary to "take such action as may be appropriate to respond to the public health emergency, including making grants, providing awards for expenses, and entering into contracts and conducting and supporting investigations into the cause, treatment, or prevention" of a "significant outbreak" of infectious disease. Six weeks later, the President declared a national emergency, Proc. No. 9994, *Declaring a National Emergency Concerning the Novel Coronavirus Disease (COVID-19) Outbreak*, 85 Fed. Reg. 15,337 (Mar. 13, 2020), which enabled him to exercise various standby statutory powers. Nevertheless, aside from 14-day quarantines for certain foreign travelers, neither authority was used by the Trump administration to restrict domestic travel or to impose mandatory constraints on individual behavior. Nor was any testing or contact tracing required.

The federal government clearly might have ordered the apprehension and examination of individuals "reasonably believed to be infected . . . and . . . moving or about to move" from one state to another. 42 U.S.C. §264(d)(1). Whether it might also have subjected infected individuals to quarantines or isolation is less clear, raising liberty issues under the Fourth and Fifth Amendments. Emily Berman, *The Roles of the State and Federal Governments in a Pandemic*, 11 J. Nat'l Security L. & Pol'y 61, 69-70 (2020). It seems very doubtful, however, that a federal quarantine could have been imposed on an entire state or region. Assuming that the statutory term "detention" encompasses quarantine or isolation, it is available only for *individuals* who are "found to be infected," 42 U.S.C. §264(d)(1), not for whole unexamined state populations. *See* Berman, *supra*, at 68-71; Goitein, *supra*, at 43. It also seems unlikely that Congress intended to authorize the federal closure of state borders when it allowed the HHS Secretary to "make and enforce such regulations as in his judgment are necessary to prevent the introduction, transmission, or spread of communicable diseases . . . from one State or possession into any other State or possession." 42 U.S.C. §264(a). *See* Goitein, *supra*, at 44. But while he threatened to do so, President Trump never sought to take any of these actions.

The CDC instead issued guidelines intended to influence a variety of activities, from social distancing to dining out, and relied on state and local officials to decide what mitigation measures to require. But actions by some high government officials appeared to undermine both the CDC's pronouncements and local government's voluntary mitigation efforts. For example, when the CDC recommended wearing masks in public, Trump declared that doing so was voluntary and that he would not do it. *See* Colin Dwyer & Allison Aubrey, *CDC Now Recommends Americans Consider Wearing Cloth Face Coverings In Public*, NPR, Apr. 3, 2020.

On his first day in office, however, President Biden ordered "Federal employees, on-site Federal contractors, and other individuals in Federal buildings and on Federal lands [to] all wear masks, maintain physical distance, and adhere to other public health measures" prescribed by the

CDC. Exec. Order No. 13,991, *Protecting the Federal Workforce and Requiring Mask-Wearing*, §1, 86 Fed. Reg. 7045, 7045 (Jan. 20, 2021). He went on to direct the HHS Secretary to "engage . . . with State, local, Tribal, and territorial officials, as well as business, union, academic, and other community leaders" to encourage public compliance with mask-wearing and other public health best practices, *id.* §3(a), but he stopped short of requiring such practices generally. In another directive the following day, however, he ordered the wearing of masks on all domestic public transportation, including buses, trains, and airplanes. Exec. Order No. 13,998, *Promoting COVID-19 Safety in Domestic and International Travel*, 86 Fed. Reg. 7205 (Jan. 21, 2021). At this writing, legal challenges to that mandate have thus far proven unsuccessful.

Why do you think the federal government has failed to act more aggressively in exercising its statutory authorities to slow the spread of the coronavirus?

c. State Restrictions

A number of states and localities have imposed mandatory restrictions on individual activities, public gatherings, businesses, or interstate travel, most commonly by executive fiat. Others have adopted only voluntary restrictions or none at all. *See* Isaac Stanley-Becker & Chelsea Janes, *As Virus Takes Hold, Resistance to Stay-at-Home Orders Remains Widespread — Exposing Political and Social Rifts*, Wash. Post, Apr. 2, 2020. There has, in short, been no uniformity in state responses to the pandemic.

State restrictions have been challenged in dozens of lawsuits in state and federal courts on a wide variety of grounds. *See* Sophie Quinton, *GOP Lawsuits Restrain Governors' COVID-19 Actions*, Pew (Nov. 17, 2020), https://www.pewtrusts.org/en/research-and-analysis/blogs/stateline/2020/11/17/goplawsuits- restrain-governors-covid-19-actions; *Lawsuits about State Actions and Policies in Response to the Coronavirus (COVID-19) Pandemic, 2020-2021*, Ballotpedia (updated regularly), https://ballotpedia.org/Lawsuits_about_state_actions_and_policies_in_response_to_the_coronavirus_(COVID-19)_pandemic,_2020-2021. Most have been dismissed. But orders from state officials to stay at home, avoid public and private gatherings, close or restrict some businesses, or regulate health care providers have notably been struck down by several state courts. *See, e.g., Midwest Inst. of Health, PLLC v. Whitmer*, 958 N.W.2d 1 (Mich. 2020) (governor lacked necessary statutory authority to impose emergency orders); *Wis. Legislature v. Palm*, 942 N.W.2d 900 (Wis.

2020) (state health official failed to satisfy statutory requirements for emergency rulemaking, and even if she had, she exceeded limits on her statutory authority).

In May 2020, the U.S. Supreme Court by a 5-4 vote narrowly refused to issue an emergency writ of injunction to block, pending appeal, a California order limiting attendance in places of worship to a maximum of 25% or 100 attendees. In a solo concurring opinion, Chief Justice Roberts wrote,

> Our Constitution principally entrusts "[t]he safety and the health of the people" to the politically accountable officials of the States "to guard and protect." *Jacobson v. Massachusetts*, 197 U.S. 11, 38 (1905). When those officials "undertake[ ] to act in areas fraught with medical and scientific uncertainties," their latitude "must be especially broad." *Marshall v. United States*, 414 U.S. 417, 427 (1974). Where those broad limits are not exceeded, they should not be subject to second-guessing by an "unelected federal judiciary," which lacks the background, competence, and expertise to assess public health and is not accountable to the people. [*South Bay United Pentecostal Church v. Newsom*, 140 S. Ct. 1613, 1613-1614 (2020) (Roberts, C.J., concurring).]

Six months later, however, the Court voted 5-4 to issue an emergency injunction to block the enforcement of a similar order by the Governor of New York to limit the size of religious services, concluding that it likely violated the Free Exercise Clause of the First Amendment. *Roman Catholic Diocese of Brooklyn v. Cuomo*, 141 S. Ct. 63 (2020) (per curiam). During the rest of the October 2020 Term, the Court would issue another five emergency injunctions against state COVID orders — all on religious liberty grounds, and most by the same 5-4 vote. *See, e.g.,* Stephen I. Vladeck, Opinion, *The Supreme Court is Making New Law in the Shadows*, N.Y. Times, Apr. 15, 2021.

What do you think accounts for this judicial about-face? Do you think the Court might have decided the latter case differently if, as in *Trump v. Hawaii*, 138 S. Ct. 2392 (2018) (NSL p. 798, CTL p. 450), the restrictive order had come instead from the President, and had been described as necessary for national security? Or can the difference be explained entirely by the change in the Court's membership between May and November — with Justice Barrett replacing Justice Ginsburg?

d. Requiring Vaccinations

In late 2020, the FDA approved the first of several COVID-19 vaccines as safe and efficacious for emergency use, and an unprecedented effort was mounted to vaccinate as many Americans as possible, in order to achieve herd immunity among the population and stop the spread of the virus. Nevertheless, many individuals have resisted vaccination, arguing that it violates constitutional rights to due process, equal protection, or the free exercise of religion; that it is dangerous; or that it offends their philosophical beliefs.

While universal vaccination has not yet been ordered by either state or federal governments, *Jacobson v. Massachusetts*, 197 U.S. 11 (1905) (upholding mandatory smallpox vaccination), and its progeny indicate that, given the contagiousness and lethality of the COVID-19 virus, a court following existing precedent would probably uphold such an order. *See* Edward P. Richards, *A Historical Review of the State Police Powers and Their Relevance to the COVID-19 Pandemic of 2020*, 11 J. Nat'l Security L. & Pol'y 83, 96-101 (2020). Could the federal government enforce such an order, despite the fact that no statute explicitly authorizes it? How might the recent trend toward politically and ideologically based opposition to vaccines in general, and the COVID-19 vaccine in particular, impact the way that courts answer this question?

If the federal government does have this authority, would that authority preempt contradictory state laws or regulations? Texas Governor Greg Abbot issued an executive order banning state agencies, political subdivisions, and organizations that receive public funds from requiring proof of COVID-19 vaccination in order to receive services. The Texas legislature then passed a law that similarly restricts businesses licensed by the state. *See* Karen Brooks Harper, *Gov. Greg Abbott Signs Bill to Punish Businesses that Require Proof of COVID-19 Vaccination*, Texas Trib., June 7, 2021. And at least one state, Florida, has enacted legislation that imposes criminal penalties on any school or business that requires proof of vaccination. Mary Ellen Klas, *DeSantis Declares Covid "State of Emergency" Over, Overrides Local Restrictions*, Miami Herald, May 3, 2021.

Could either federal or state governments order vaccination of only part of the population, such as health care providers, law enforcement officers, or teachers, who have close contact with the public? May colleges and universities require vaccinations as a condition of enrollment? On what legal basis, if any, may employers require vaccination as a condition of employment? After a federal judge rejected a challenge to Houston's Methodist Hospital policy requiring all employees to be vaccinated, 153 employees resigned or were fired pursuant to the policy. *See* Dan Diamond, *153 People Resigned or Were Fired from a Texas Hospital System After Refusing to Get Vaccinated*, Wash. Post, June 22, 2021.

1.2. Privacy in the Time of COVID? The terrorist attacks of 9/11 prompted extensive new government efforts to collect, store, and analyze non-public personal information. Some of these efforts are still secret or at least not fully understood. Two decades later, the resulting tradeoffs between privacy and security continue to be vigorously debated. Serious questions about statutory authority for these efforts, and about their constitutionality, are analyzed elsewhere in the casebook.

Government collection of personal information in response to the COVID-19 pandemic may raise some of the same concerns about personal privacy.

> Health surveillance in response to a pandemic, however, has a very different goal. The primary purpose is to educate and inform — to let people know where there are large numbers of people congregating so that they can take steps to avoid what might become the next disease hot spot; to tell individuals that they have been in close contact with someone deemed contagious; to make visible and transparent the need to test and self-quarantine; to let those subject to quarantine orders know that their movements are being monitored in order to induce compliance. [Jennifer Daskal, *Good Health and Good Privacy Go Hand-in-Hand*, 11 J. Nat'l Security L. & Pol'y 131, 132 (2020).]

In a number of countries around the world, governments have used cell phone data, credit card information, and facial recognition technology to monitor the movements of quarantined or isolated persons, or to perform contract-tracing. They have also relied on personal health records to identify and locate infected individuals.

In the United States, however, such information has generally been collected by state and federal officials only with the consent of the individuals concerned. That could change if, for example, some state governments refused to cooperate in nationwide efforts to stem the spread of the virus, or if a COVID-19 variant threatened a new pandemic.

Do you think federal officials could order mandatory health screenings for everyone in the United States, relying on provisions of the Public Health Service Act described above? Could screenings be required for certain activities, such as admission to sports events, or for employment in particular jobs, such as nursing home care? Could proof of vaccination for COVID-19 be required for any of these activities — in light of the fact that such a precondition would effectively impose not only a duty to disclose personal information but also an affirmative obligation to undergo an invasive medical procedure?

May the federal government collect personal information about infected individuals from health care providers, employers, or testing services without a warrant? The Supreme Court's decision in *Carpenter v. United States*, 138 S. Ct. 2206 (2018) (NSL p. 685, CTL p. 337), raised serious doubts about the continued viability of the "third-party" doctrine, especially as it might be invoked in this context to gather electronic records to trace individual movements. But could such collection be justified by the Court's "special needs" exception to the Fourth Amendment's warrant requirement (see NSL pp. 580, 638; CTL pp. 232, 290), assuming the data were used for public health rather than law enforcement purposes, given the extreme danger posed by the continued spread of the virus?

If the government were justified in collecting such personal data, what, if anything, could be done with that information, aside from tracking the movements of infected individuals and noting their contacts with others? Could any of the data be shared with the persons contacted? Could the information be shared among government agencies, state and local as well as federal, without violating the constraints of the Privacy Act of 1974, 5 U.S.C. §552a (2018) (described briefly at NSL p. 1273)?

Could concerns about the reasonableness of government surveillance under the Fourth Amendment be allayed by the anonymization of any personal data collected? *See* Ira S. Rubinstein & Woodrow Hartzog, *Anonymization & Risk*, 91 Wash. L. Rev. 703 (2016) (outlining potential weaknesses of such precautions). What about a limit on the time that such data could be retained to, say, a 14-day latency period? Or an express limitation on the use of the data to the purpose for which it was collected? Would you favor government collection, retention, and use of personal health information if accompanied by rigorous oversight and accounting procedures to prevent its misuse? Can you describe such procedures?

———————

[NSL p. 1180, CTL p. 832. Insert above the ruled line near the top of the page.]

§265. SUSPENSION OF ENTRIES AND IMPORTS FROM DESIGNATED PLACES TO PREVENT SPREAD OF COMMUNICABLE DISEASES

Whenever the Surgeon General determines that by reason of the existence of any communicable disease in a foreign country there is serious danger of the introduction of such disease into the United States . . . the Surgeon General . . . shall have the power to prohibit, in whole or in part, the introduction of persons and property from such countries or places as he shall designate in order to avert such danger, and for such period of time as he may deem necessary for such purpose.

[NSL p. 1182, CTL p. 834. Insert after Note 4.]

4.1. Federalism in the Time of COVID. When the COVID-19 pandemic struck the nation in 2020, one of us offered this observation:

> As a public health matter, the primary responsibility for pandemic response lies with the states. At the same time, multiple laws, policies, and the numerous pandemic-response plans that the federal government has developed make plain that a successful fight against an outbreak of the scale and severity of COVID-19 requires a national response, with significant responsibilities necessarily falling on the federal government. [Emily Berman, *The Roles of the State and Federal Governments in a Pandemic*, 11 J. Nat'l Security L. & Pol'y 61, 62 (2020).]

But instead of a contest for power, "[s]tate leaders have consistently pleaded for more active federal leadership — more policy guidance, more material resources, more national coordination." *Id.*

Historically, states have played a lead role in responding to outbreaks of contagious diseases like smallpox, tuberculosis, and HIV. *See* Edward P. Richards, *A Historical Review of the State Police Powers and Their Relevance to the COVID-19 Pandemic of 2020*, 11 J. Nat'l Security L. & Pol'y 83 (2020). Nevertheless, some responsibilities fall inevitably to the federal government, including detection and reporting of infections, forecasting how a disease will spread and what its impact will be, development of tests, treatments, and vaccines, stockpiling supplies, and securing of supply chains for critical equipment — all tasks beyond the capabilities of individual states.

Early in 2020, every state declared a public health emergency, giving governors and local officials extraordinary regulatory powers. Yet while many states imposed stringent limits on businesses and individuals, some even barring nonessential travel across state lines without quarantine upon entry, regulations in others were far less intrusive. Some states refused to require mask wearing or to limit public gatherings, or having adopted such restrictions they lifted them after a short time. Because the COVID-19 virus is so easily transmitted among humans, and because it does not respect political boundaries, it quickly spread from coast to coast.

When a number of state governors announced in April 2020 that they would coordinate plans to lift COVID-19 restrictions and reopen their economies, President Trump protested that they lacked the authority to do so. "I have the ultimate authority," he declared. "When somebody is the president of the United States, the authority is total and that's the way it's got to be. . . . It's total. The governors know that." Meagan Flynn & Allyson Chiu, *Trump Says His "Authority Is Total." Constitutional Experts Have "No Idea" Where He Got That*, Wash. Post, Apr. 14, 2020. Another one of us responded, "Nope. That would be the literal definition of a 'totalitarian' government — which our traditions, our Constitution, and our values all rightly and decisively reject." *Id.*

If the President's authority in this context is less than total, can you confidently describe its limits? Is he empowered, for example, to order schools and restaurants either to close or to reopen? Could he override state government directives to the contrary?

———————

[NSL p. 1182, CTL p. 834. Insert after Note 5.]

5.1. Supplies to Combat COVID-19. Evaluating the government's preparedness for the COVID-19 pandemic, FEMA found "insufficient resources to meet national demands," noting "global shortages of PPE [personal protective equipment] and testing kits." FEMA, *Pandemic Response to Coronavirus Disease 2019 (COVID-19): Initial Assessment Report* 8 (Jan. 13, 2021).

Once the pandemic got underway, these resources might have been more widely available if President Trump had made full use of the Defense Production Act of 1950 (DPA), 50 U.S.C. §§4501-4568 (2018), to require the manufacture and sale to the federal government of items in short supply. But at the urging of the U.S. Chamber of Commerce and others, Trump invoked the Act, then relied on it primarily to encourage voluntary industry responses to critical needs. *See* James E. Baker, *From*

Shortages to Stockpiles: How the Defense Production Act Can Be Used to Save Lives, Make America the Global Arsenal of Public Health, and Address the Security Challenges Ahead, 11 J. Nat'l Security L. & Pol'y 157 (2020); Elizabeth Goitein, *Emergency Powers, Real and Imagined: How President Trump Used and Failed to Use Presidential Authority in the COVID-19 Crisis,* 11 J. Nat'l Security L. & Pol'y 27, 60-64 (2020); *see also* Michael H. Cecire & Heidi M. Peters, *The Defense Production Act of 1950: History, Authorities, and Considerations for Congress* (Cong. Res. Serv. R43767), Mar. 2, 2020; Michael H. Cecire et al., *COVID-19 and Domestic PPE Production and Distribution: Issues and Policy Options* (Cong. Res. Serv. R46628), Dec. 7, 2020.

Existing pandemic-response plans call for active federal government supply chain management and supply distribution to ensure that available resources reach the locations where they are most needed, and the DPA confers authority on the federal government to play this role. 50 U.S.C. §4511(a)(2). But President Trump failed to use this authority to allocate critically short supplies among the states, declaring instead that it was the responsibility of states, not the federal government, to acquire these resources for themselves. *See* Quint Forgey, *"We're Not a Shipping Clerk": Trump Tells Governors to Step up Efforts to Get Medical Supplies,* Politico, Mar. 19, 2020; Jeanne Whalen et al., *Scramble for Medical Equipment Descends into Chaos as U.S. States and Hospitals Compete for Rare Supplies,* Wash. Post, Mar. 24, 2020.

The federal government was also reluctant to distribute the contents of the Strategic National Stockpile, which held a multi-billion-dollar inventory of drugs, vaccines, medical devices, personal protective equipment, and diagnostic tests. Before the pandemic struck, HHS described the stockpile as being used in public health emergencies "severe enough to cause local supplies to run out." In April 2020, however, the official online description was altered to describe its role as "to supplement state and local supplies during public health emergencies," while pointing out that "states have products stockpiled, as well." Quint Forgey, *Strategic National Stockpile Description Altered Online after Kushner's Remarks,* Politico, Apr. 3, 2020.

When vaccines for the coronavirus began to be approved by the FDA in late 2020, a new challenge arose: rapid and equitable distribution of the vaccines to inoculate Americans. (Legal and ethical questions about making limited supplies of vaccines available to the rest of the world were largely ignored initially, even though the virus will continue to pose a threat to the United States until enough of the global population is vaccinated to achieve herd immunity. *See, e.g., UN Expert Says Global Coordination and More Equitable Sharing of COVID-19 Vaccines Key to Recovery*, Off. of the High Commissioner, U.N. Human Rts. (Jan. 22, 2021)). But while the government invested large sums (with some drug companies, but not others) to finance the development and manufacture of COVID-19 vaccines, their initial allocation to states was chaotic and unpredictable.

One federal statute provides that the HHS Secretary, "together with relevant manufacturers, wholesalers, and distributors as may agree to cooperate, may track the initial distribution of federally purchased influenza vaccine in an influenza pandemic." 42 U.S.C. §247d-1(a) (2018 & Supp. I 2019). Whether any such tracking was done, or how it might have influenced government actions, is unclear.

Once vaccines began to reach the states, the Trump administration made no effort, aside from CDC recommendations, to regulate the vaccination of individuals within states. *See* Ctrs. for Disease Control & Prevention, *CDC's COVID-19 Vaccine Rollout Recommendations* (Feb. 3, 2021). Varying priorities were set by states — some making vaccines available first to health care providers and nursing home residents, for example, others to persons above a certain age. *See Coronavirus Restrictions and Mask Mandates for All 50 States*, N.Y. Times (updated regularly).

Shortly after taking office, President Biden directed federal agencies to take "immediate actions to secure supplies necessary for responding to the pandemic," utilizing the DPA to fill shortfalls if needed, and to plan for the distribution of PPE and vaccines. Exec. Order No. 14,001, *A Sustainable Public Health Supply Chain*, 86 Fed. Reg. 7219 (Jan. 21, 2021).

Do you think the federal government should interfere with market forces to procure medical equipment and supplies, including vaccines, needed to combat a pandemic? Should it regulate distribution of such materials among the states? Should the federal government establish mandatory priorities for vaccinations? Is the President currently authorized to set such priorities?

[NSL p. 1190, CTL p. 842. Add to the last paragraph of Note 3.]

In a case arising out of the law enforcement response to demonstrations in Lafayette Square on June 1, 2020, the court declared that "there is no justification for finding that Congress intended the statute to include an extra-textual civil remedy," although no military forces covered by the PCA were involved. *Black Lives Matter D.C. v. Trump*, No. 20-cv-1469, 2021 WL 2530722, at *13 (D.D.C. June 21, 2021).

[NSL p. 1194, CTL p. 846. Add to Note 2.]

After the killing of George Floyd by Minneapolis police officers on May 25, 2020, protests broke out around the country. For the most part these demonstrations were peaceful, although there were sporadic instances of arson, looting, and vandalism. On June 1, President Trump responded this way:

> Today, I have strongly recommended to every governor to deploy the National Guard in sufficient numbers that we dominate the streets. Mayors and governors must establish an overwhelming law enforcement presence until the violence has been quelled.
>
> If a city or a state refuses to take the actions that are necessary to defend the life and property of their residents, then I will deploy the United States military and quickly solve the problem for them. [Scott R. Anderson & Michel Paradis, *Can Trump Use the Insurrection Act to Deploy Troops to American Streets?*, Lawfare, June 3, 2020.]

White House officials reportedly drafted a proclamation to invoke the Insurrection Act in order to enable deployment of federal troops for law enforcement in cities around the country. But upon the advice of the Attorney General, Defense Secretary, and Joint Chiefs chair, Trump reluctantly decided not to invoke the Act. *See* Michael S. Schmidt & Maggie Haberman, *Trump Weighed Insurrection Act Amid Protests*, N.Y. Times, June 26, 2020.

In addition to the statutory text excerpted above, the Insurrection Act permits the President to use the military in a state to suppress "any insurrection, domestic violence, unlawful combination, or conspiracy" that

> (1) so hinders the execution of the laws of that State, and of the United States within the State, that any part or class of its people is deprived of a right, privilege, immunity, or protection named in the Constitution and secured by law, and the constituted authorities of that State are unable, fail, or refuse to protect that right, privilege, or immunity, or to give that protection; . . . . [10 U.S.C. §253.]

Most of the demonstrations in mid-2020 were non-violent. Those that were not were quickly contained by local authorities, sometimes aided by unfederalized National Guard troops. Nevertheless, some of the protestors appeared to violate federal laws that address travel across state lines to engage in rioting, the use of weapons, and injury to government property. *See* Peter G. Berris & Michael A. Foster, *Federal Criminal Laws Applicable to Rioting, Property Destruction, and Related Conduct*

(Cong. Res. Serv. LSB10493), June 11, 2020. Could Trump have relied on any part of the Insurrection Act to justify deployment of "the United States military" in a state over the objection of its governor? If you doubt that he could have done so, do you think a court would have ordered him to stop? *See* Anderson & Paradis, *supra* (suggesting that the answer to both questions is no).

———————

[NSL p. 1207, CTL p. 859. Add before Notes and Questions.]

5. A Military Role in Elections?

A strong background principle in the United States holds that the military should avoid involvement in civil affairs, especially elections. In the leadup to the November 2020 presidential election, however, there was widespread concern about possible acts of violence on election day aimed at disrupting operations at the polls. More than 3,600 unfederalized National Guard troops were activated by various state governors ahead of Election Day 2020 to guard against such disruptions.

There was also concern that President Trump might use threats or isolated acts of violence as a pretext to send active-duty military or federalized National Guard troops to polling places in an effort to influence the election. *See* Jennifer Steinhauer & Helene Cooper, *At Pentagon, Fears Grow That Trump Will Pull Military into Election Unrest*, N.Y. Times, Sept. 25, 2020. Speculation along these lines was sufficiently widespread that Gen. Mark Milley, Chairman of the Joint Chiefs of Staff, announced to both Congress and the media that "if there's a disputed election, that'll be handled by Congress and the courts. There's no role for the U.S. military in determining the outcome of a U.S. election. Zero, there is no role there." Missy Ryan, *As Election Nears, Pentagon Leaders' Goal of Staying Out of Elections Is Tested*, Wash. Post, Oct. 14, 2020.

These election-related issues implicate at least three provisions of the U.S. Code. Title 18 U.S.C §592 bars members of the military from deployment anywhere an election is being held, "unless such force be necessary to repel armed enemies of the United States." Title 18 U.S.C. §593 prohibits members of the armed forces from imposing rules regarding the conduct of an election or the qualification of voters; preventing "by force, threat, intimidation, advice or otherwise any qualified voter of any State from fully exercising the right of suffrage"; compelling state officials to allow ineligible voters to cast a ballot; or otherwise interfering with election officials. The forerunner of these two provisions was a Civil-War era measure animated by fear that President Lincoln would use the military or civil service to prevent his opponents from voting. Finally, 18 U.S.C. §594 forbids anyone, military or civilian, from intimidating voters for the purpose of interfering with or affecting the content of their vote.

The Posse Comitatus Act also has implications for the military's possible role in elections. In the presidential election of 1876, President Ulysses S. Grant sent soldiers to polling places in three Southern states to assist federal marshals as *posses comitatus* to protect former slaves seeking to exercise their right to vote under the newly ratified Fifteenth Amendment. He was expressly authorized to do so by the 1870 Enforcement Act, 16 Stat. 140, and the Ku Klux Act of 1871, 17 Stat. 13. When Rutherford B. Hayes defeated Samuel Tilden by one electoral vote (but lost the popular vote) in that election, aggrieved Democrats agreed not to contest the outcome if Hayes would withdraw all remaining federal forces from former Confederate states, ending Reconstruction. Two years later, Southern Democrats forced passage of the Posse Comitatus Act, barring the use of troops for law enforcement unless expressly permitted by statute or the Constitution. The Enforcement Act of 1870 and the Ku Klux Act, now incorporated in part in the Insurrection Act, were statutory exceptions.

6. A Military Role in Protecting the U.S. Capitol and Congress?

While Election Day 2020 passed without any significant acts of violence, questions about the role of the military arose again on January 6, 2021, when Congress convened to officially tally the votes of the Electoral College that would make Joseph R. Biden the next President. As the vote-counting got underway that day, the U.S. Capitol was surrounded by thousands of supporters of President Donald Trump who sought to prevent Congress from completing the count and officially announcing the results of the election. Some 800 of the demonstrators broke into the Capitol building, where they forced an adjournment of both Houses, threatened the Vice President and Members of Congress, and did extensive damage. Capitol and D.C. police were completely overwhelmed.

At 1:49 p.m., just minutes before rioters entered the Capitol, the Capitol Police chief urgently requested help from National Guard personnel who were waiting in buses nearby. Earlier that same week, however, any such deployment had been barred without approval by the Acting Defense Secretary and the Secretary of the Army. Approval came more than three hours later, at 5:08 p.m. When Guard troops finally arrived , the rioters had already begun to disperse.

Suspicions immediately arose that the Pentagon's lengthy delay in approving the deployment of Guard troops was politically motivated. *See, e.g.,* Dana Milbank, *Did the Pentagon Wait for Trump's Approval Before Defending the Capitol?*, Wash. Post, Mar. 3, 2021. At least two congressional committees have held hearings seeking explanations for the delay. A bipartisan Senate report issued in June 2021 described failures by the FBI, DHS, and Capitol Police to share intelligence about or plan for the violent attack. It also reported confusion in communications, inexplicable dithering by DOD officials, and much finger-pointing. U.S. Sen. Comms. on Homeland Security & Gov't Affairs and Rules & Admin., *Examining the U.S. Capitol Attack: A Review of the Security, Planning, and Response Failures on January 6* (2021), https://www.rules.senate.gov/download/hsgac-rules-jan-6-report. The report concluded,

> January 6, 2021 marked not only an attack on the Capitol Building — it marked an attack on democracy. The entities responsible for securing and protecting the Capitol Complex and everyone onsite that day were not prepared for a large-scale attack, despite being aware of the potential for violence targeting the Capitol." [*Id.* at 95.]

Senate Republicans blocked the creation of an independent commission, modeled on the 9/11 Commission, to investigate the events of January 6. *See* Karoun Demirjian, *GOP Senators Block Jan. 6 Commission, Likely Ending Bid for Independent Probe of Capitol Riot*, Wash. Post, May 28, 2021. The House of Representatives will instead task a select committee to investigate what happened and why, and how to prevent similar incidents in the future. *See* Felicia Sonmez & Karoun Demirjiam, *Pelosi Announces a Select Committee Will Investigate Jan. 6 Attack on the Capitol by a Pro-Trump Mob,* Wash. Post., June 24, 2021.

In the aftermath of the rioting, several thousand National Guard troops from the District of Columbia and five states were mobilized to provide security in and around Washington, D.C. and the Capitol. Barbara Starr & Devan Cole, *Nearly 6,200 National Guard Are Being Mobilized to Provide Security to DC Following Capitol Riot*, CNN, Jan. 7, 2021. Another 20,000 Guard personnel from around the country were deployed during the inauguration of President Joe Biden, and some of these remained in the District, at the request of the Capitol Police, until the end of May. *See* Amanda Macias, *National Guard Troops Leave Capitol Months After Deadly Jan. 6 Insurrection*, CNBC, May 24, 2021.

7. Security Without Representation — The Special Role of the D.C. National Guard

Deployment of troops from the D.C. National Guard during the January 6, 2021 Capitol insurrection and thereafter underscores certain unique features of its command structure. The District of Columbia is, of course, not a state or territory, and, by statute, the President of the United States is commander in chief of its military forces. D.C. Code §49-409 (2020). The President has delegated the authority to activate the D.C. Guard to the Secretary of Defense, who has in turn handed that job over to the Secretary of the Army. *See District of Columbia National Guard* (n.d.), https://dc.ng.mil/About-Us/.

The D.C. mayor has no direct authority over the District's National Guard. But this provision of the D.C. Code, which is federal law, is clearly relevant to the events of January 6:

> When there is in the District of Columbia a tumult, riot, mob, or a body of men acting together by force with attempt to commit a felony or to offer violence to persons or property, or by force or violence to break and resist the laws, or when such tumult, riot, or mob is threatened, it shall be lawful for the Mayor of the District of Columbia . . . to call on the Commander-in-Chief to aid them in suppressing such violence and enforcing the laws; the Commander-in-Chief shall thereupon order out so much and such portion of the militia as he may deem necessary to suppress the same . . . . [D.C. Code §49-103 (2020).]

On January 4, 2021, Acting Defense Secretary Miller approved a request from D.C. Mayor Muriel Bowser to use some 340 unarmed D.C. Guard troops for "crowd management" and traffic control in anticipation of the pro-Trump rally scheduled two days later. Alex Marquardt et al., *Pentagon Approves DC Mayor's Request to Deploy National Guard for Upcoming Demonstrations*, CNN, Jan. 4, 2021. But on January 6, when the Capitol Police chief urgently called for aid from Guard troops to suppress the riot, approval was delayed for more than three hours. Whether President Trump was involved in the approval process is unclear.

Other distinctions mark the D.C. National Guard, as well. So long as its forces are not federalized by the President under the Insurrection Act, it, like other National Guard units, operates free of the constraints of the Posse Comitatus Act. Unlike other Guard units, however, the Justice Department has taken the position that it may be used *by the President* for law enforcement within the District of Columbia without invoking the Insurrection Act. *Use of the National Guard to Support Drug*

Interdiction Efforts in the District of Columbia, 13 Op. O.L.C. 91 (1989). Thus, for example, some 200 D.C. Guard personnel played a prominent role in the widely criticized expulsion of peaceful protesters from Lafayette Square on June 1, 2020. Moreover, according to the strict terms of the Insurrection Act, deployment of D.C. Guard forces outside the District for law enforcement would require invocation of 10 U.S.C. §253, not §251 or §252, which refer only to militias of "states." (Indeed, 10 U.S.C. §255 conspicuously omits the District of Columbia — but not Guam or the U.S. Virgin Islands — from the Insurrection Act's definition of "state").

The D.C. National Guard is quite small, with only about 2,700 soldiers and airmen. To augment those numbers, in the summer of 2020 President Trump, unbeknownst to D.C. local officials, requested various states to voluntarily send their National Guard troops — in Title 32 status — to help control demonstrations in the District. Governors from eleven states sent about 4,000 soldiers (10 of the governors were Republicans). Others refused. The borrowed forces performed various law enforcement-like tasks, including "crowd control, temporary detention, cursory search, measures to ensure the safety of persons on the property, and establishment of security perimeters." Steve Vladeck, *Why Were Out-of-State National Guard Units in Washington, D.C.? The Justice Department's Troubling Explanation,* Lawfare, June 9, 2020 (questioning the applicability of 32 U.S.C. §502(f)). Should Congress consider limiting such an obvious end-run around the Posse Comitatus Act by subjecting National Guard troops in Title 32 status to the 1878 law? Should Congress at least require the consent not only of the Governor who *sends* troops, but of the Governor (or, for D.C., Mayor) into whose territory they are being deployed?

8. A Military Role in Pandemics?

Like its civilian counterparts, the military anticipated the need to respond to pandemic infectious disease, both at home and abroad. In the years after 9/11, the Department of Defense generated numerous policies to guide its response. *See, e.g.,* Dep't of Defense, *Global Campaign Plan for Pandemic Influenza and Infectious Disease 3551-13* (2013). Northern Command even has a 2017 draft plan (apparently never officially adopted) noting that national strategic threats "may include severe economic, political, and social consequences both domestically and internationally," and that there would likely be insufficient supply of critical resources, such as "ventilators, devices, personal protective equipment such as face masks and gloves." *See* U.S. Northern

Command, *CONPLAN 3560, Pandemic Influenza and Infectious Disease Response, NORTHCOM Branch Plan 3560* (draft Jan. 6, 2017), at C-1-D-11. These plans envision the military's primary domestic responsibility as supporting civilian agencies on the front lines of the fight against disease.

The military did, in fact, provide some resources to assist in the domestic COVID-19 response. Early in the course of the pandemic, when numbers of cases threatened to overwhelm civilian health care systems, the Army Corps of Engineers constructed field hospitals in parking lots, stadiums, and convention centers around the country. In March 2020, the Navy deployed two hospital ships, the USNS *Comfort* to New York and the USNS *Mercy* to Los Angeles, to alleviate overcrowding in local hospitals. In addition, hundreds of medical professionals from the Army, Navy, and Air Force deployed to bolster COVID-19-related health care efforts in Texas and California.

Upon taking office, the Biden administration promised to vaccinate 100 million Americans for COVID-19 in his first 100 days in office — a number the President subsequently revised to 150 million. FEMA asked the Pentagon to deploy as many as 10,000 active-duty troops and National Guard personnel to help in this effort. By mid-February, more than 4,700 soldiers in 25 teams were on their way to sites around the country. Eleanor Watson & Nicole Sganga, *Pentagon Authorizes More Troops to Assist with Vaccination Effort*, CBS News, Feb. 15, 2021.

The White House also directed FEMA to reimburse states for use of their National Guard troops to assist with vaccinations. *President Biden Announces Increased Vaccine Supply, Initial Launch of the Federal Retail Pharmacy Program, and Expansion of FEMA Reimbursement to States*, Feb. 2, 2021. And the Defense Department provided transportation for the Department of Health and Human Services in importing needles and syringes, 80 percent of which come from China.

[NSL p. 1208, CTL p. 860. Insert at the end of Note 4.]

Soon after taking office, President Biden ended a national emergency declared earlier by President Trump that purported to justify, in part, the deployment of troops on the U.S.-Mexico border. Proc. No. 10,142, *Termination of Emergency With Respect to the Southern Border of the United States and Redirection of Funds Diverted to Border Wall Construction*, 86 Fed. Reg. 7467 (Jan. 20, 2021), reversing Proc. No. 9844, *Declaring a National Emergency Concerning the Southern Border of the United States*, 84 Fed. Reg. 4949 (Feb. 15, 2019) (NSL p. 70). The

Pentagon said it had no plans to immediately redeploy some 3,600 troops, both active-duty and National Guard, who remained there, and the Department of Homeland Security requested their continued support of border operations for an additional extended period. *See* W.J. Hennigan, *The National Emergency at U.S-Mexico Border Is Over. But Thousands of Troops Remain*, Time, Feb. 11, 2021; Rose L. Thayer, *Troops at US-Mexico Border Could Stay There for Three to Five Years, Report Says*, Stars and Stripes, Feb. 25, 2021.

[NSL p. 1208, CTL p. 860. Insert after Note 4.]

5. Troops at the Polls? Federal troops are barred from deployment at polling places, except to "repel armed enemies of the United States." 18 U.S.C. §592. Who qualifies as an "armed enemy"? Does the term include domestic militias like the violent, far-right Proud Boys? Should it matter that President Trump encouraged such militias to locate themselves at the polls on election day for "voter protection"?

Voter intimidation and other forms of election interference by military personnel are explicitly prohibited by 18 U.S.C. §593. Would at least some voters not inevitably be intimidated by the presence of soldiers at the polls? If so, might troops be used to monitor activity at polling places through remote means, such as drones or cyber operations, so long as they were not physically present? Do the prohibitions on military presence extend to vote tabulation after the polls close? What about subsequent meetings of state electors to cast electoral college ballots or sessions of Congress to count the electoral votes?

In December 2020, based on the false premise that the 2020 presidential election was marred by widespread fraud, President Trump's former National Security Advisor, Gen. Michael Flynn, suggested that the President could use troops to seize voting machines in several swing states and rerun elections there. Solange Reyner, *Michael Flynn to Newsmax TV: Trump Has Options to Secure Integrity of 2020 Election*, Newmax, Dec. 17, 2020. Was Flynn correct? Would your answer be different if there had in fact been a conspiracy to commit widespread election fraud, thereby hindering the execution of state election laws and potentially disenfranchising millions of voters? If so, who should determine whether the requisite conspiracy existed?

6. Troops at the U.S. Capitol? DOD regulations long asserted a right of military forces, based in the Constitution, to take "prompt and vigorous Federal action . . . to prevent loss of life or wanton destruction of property and to restore governmental functioning" when "sudden and unexpected civil disturbances" overwhelm local authorities. *See* NSL p. 1195, CTL p. 847. Similarly, a DOD directive gives military commanders "immediate response authority" or "emergency authority" to act to save lives or prevent great property damage when "time does not permit approval from higher authority." DOD Dir. No. 3025.18, *Defense Support of Civil Authorities (DSCA)* (Dec. 29, 2010, with Change 2 Mar. 19, 2018). See NSL p. 1204, CTL p. 856. Should these authorities have been invoked by the commander of the D.C. National Guard on January 6, 2020, to deploy his troops immediately, instead of waiting for Pentagon approval?

Do you think Guard soldiers should be used to provide ongoing security in and around the U.S. Capitol? Can you point to authority for such use?

7. *The D.C. National Guard.* When protests for racial justice in the District of Columbia grew larger and occasionally violent in June 2020, why do you think President Trump failed to invoke the Insurrection Act to allow D.C. National Guard troops to preserve order? Why did he not do so to bring in Guard forces from a number of states?

When National Guard troops from various states arrived in the District, it was not entirely clear what functions they would perform or whether they would be commanded by state or federal authorities. Because they served in Title 32 status, they technically were commanded by their respective state governors. But confusion arose when Defense Secretary Mark Esper "ordered" the out-of-state Guard troops not to use firearms or ammunition without consulting the White House. Paul Sonne, Fenit Nirappil & Josh Dawsey, *Pentagon Disarms National Guard Activated in D.C., Sends Active-Duty Forces Home*, Wash. Post, June 5, 2020. If the distinction between Title 32 status and Title 10 status for Guard forces is thus blurred, how, if at all, will their actions be constrained by the Posse Comitatus Act? How could any confusion on this important point be avoided?

8. *Troops in a Pandemic?* Several federal statutes authorize the deployment of U.S. troops in other countries for "humanitarian" assistance, including medical care. *See, e.g.,* 10 U.S.C. §401 (reproduced at NSL p. 472). But no clearly comparable statutory authority exists for domestic deployments. If the President is permitted to employ military personnel to provide health care and administer vaccines, may he also use them for other purposes related to a pandemic, such as the enforcement of curfews, stay-at-home orders, and quarantines? What

about using military resources to collect and share personal data for the purpose of contact tracing?

[NSL p. 1212, CTL p. 864. Insert after Note 4.]

5. *A Proposed Coup d'Etat?* Frustrated by Donald Trump's defeat in the 2020 election, and repeating the former President's unsubstantiated claim that the election of President Biden resulted from widespread voter fraud, former National Security Advisor Michael T. Flynn (a retired Army 3-star general) proposed invoking martial law to force new elections in swing states, then indicated support for a military overthrow of the democratically elected government. "I mean, it should happen here," he stated before a large crowd. Maggie Astor, *Michael Flynn Suggested at a QAnon-Affiliated Event That a Coup Should Happen in the U.S.*, N.Y. Times, June 1, 2021. (He later claimed that he didn't mean what he said.)

Flynn's statement came as polls showed that millions of Americans also believed that the 2020 presidential election was "stolen," and that Trump could be "reinstated" as President later in 2021. Annie Karni & Maggie Haberman, *At Once Diminished and Dominating, Trump Begins His Next Act*, N.Y. Times, June 5, 2021. His former high military rank and government position raised serious concerns about the possible influence of his remark.

Title 18 U.S.C. §2385 (2018) provides that "[w]hoever knowingly or willfully advocates, abets, advises, or teaches the duty, necessity, desirability, or propriety of overthrowing or destroying the government of the United States . . . by force or violence . . . [s]hall be fined under this title or imprisoned not more than twenty years." Do you think Flynn could or should face criminal prosecution for his statement?

Flynn's comment also sparked a lively debate regarding whether the retired three-star general could (and should) be subject to a court martial for his statements. *Compare* Eugene R. Fidell, *Getting Real About General Flynn*, Just Security, June 7, 2021 (expressing skepticism that Flynn's comments meet the definition of any punishable offense and questioning whether assertion of court-martial jurisdiction over retirees is constitutional), *with* Tom Boggioni, *Michael Flynn Should Be Sitting in Prison Awaiting Trial for Sedition: Former White House Attorney*, Salon, June 1, 2021 (noting former White House counsel Richard Painter's opinion that Flynn should be prosecuted in either civilian or military courts for sedition). For differing answers to whether the Constitution permits the court-martial of retired servicemembers for offenses committed while retired, compare *United States v. Begani*, No. 20-0217/NA, 2021 WL 2639319 (C.A.A.F. June 24, 2021) ("yes") with *Larrabee v. Braithwaite*, 502 F. Supp. 3d 322 (D.D.C. 2020) ("no"), *appeal docketed*, No. 21-5012 (D.C. Cir.).

[NSL p. 1226. Insert after the third full paragraph.]

For many years, former Presidents have continued to receive intelligence briefings and access to classified information after leaving office, enabling them to serve as emissaries or offer advice about future developments. Doubts arose about extending such access to former President Trump, however, because of his reported refusal to fully or regularly read the President's Daily Brief, his persistent dismissal of information from the intelligence community, and his history of publicly disclosing highly classified information (see casebook p. 1252). Some also worried about secret communications by Trump and members of his administration with Russia and about foreign business entanglements that might make him vulnerable to the nation's adversaries. *See* Susan M. Gordon, Opinion, *A Former President Trump Won't "Need to Know." Cut Off His Intelligence*, Wash. Post, Jan. 15, 2021.

Shortly after President Biden took office, he declared that Trump should not continue to receive intelligence briefings, citing the former President's "erratic behavior." Kathryn Watson, *Biden Says "No Need" for Trump to Still Receive Intel Briefings*, CBS News, Feb. 6, 2021. "What value is giving him an intelligence briefing?" Biden asked. "What impact does he have at all, other than the fact he might slip and say something?" *Id.*

Because a President needs no security clearance, he also need not sign an agreement not to disclose classified information (see below). If President Biden can cut off his predecessor's continuing access to classified information, can he do anything to prevent the former President's disclosure of information obtained while he was still in office? *See* Shane Harris, *As an Ex-president, Trump Could Disclose the Secrets He Learned While in Office, Current and Former Officials Fear*, Wash. Post, Nov. 10, 2020 (suggesting that Trump's "ignorance may be the best counterweight to the risk he poses").

[NSL p. 1228. Insert at the end of Note 1.]

They complained specifically about delays in review, and about denial of permission to publish information obtained from public sources or relating to issues or events that arose after they left government service. They also worried that demands for redactions might be based on policy disputes or agency embarrassment. The court rejected their challenge, concluding that agency review procedures were neither void for vagueness under the First and Fifth Amendments, nor "unreasonable" as prior restraints on publication, citing *Snepp v. United States*, 444 U.S. 507 (1980). 454 F. Supp. 3d 502 (D. Md. 2020), *aff'd sub nom. Edgar v. Haines*, No. 20-1568, 2021 WL 2557893 (4th Cir. June 23, 2021).

[NSL p. 1234. Replace the last sentence of the carryover paragraph with the following.]

Snowden failed to submit his manuscript for review, preferring, according to his lawyer, "to risk his future royalties [rather] than to subject his experiences to improper government censorship." Mihir Zaveri, *U.S. Entitled to Edward Snowden's Proceeds from His New Memoir, Judge Says*, N.Y. Times, Dec. 18, 2019. Responding to the government's motion for summary judgment, Snowden offered affirmative defenses that the government would not have conducted a review in good faith and within a reasonable time, and that the suit was prompted by animus toward his viewpoint and selective enforcement. The court rejected Snowden's request for discovery on these issues, noting that he could have litigated them if a review had turned out unfavorably. *United States v. Snowden*, No. 1:19-cv-1197, 2019 WL 8333546, at *5 (E.D. Va. Dec. 17, 2019). The court then imposed a constructive trust on Snowden's profits.

[NSL p. 1234. Insert after the first full paragraph.]

Before former National Security Advisor John Bolton published a tell-all book about his work for President Trump, *The Room Where It Happened* (2020), he submitted the manuscript for prepublication review. Bolton had signed both SF 312 and SF 4414 before joining the Trump administration. After deleting material at the insistence of an NSC reviewer, he was told that what remained included no classified information. He was not given written permission to publish, however, and he was told that the review process was ongoing. Bolton nevertheless sent the manuscript to his publisher, which printed and distributed many thousands of copies of the book around the world. The Justice Department then asked a court to order Bolton to "instruct his publisher to delay the release date of the book pending the completion of the prepublication review process" and to "take any and all available steps to retrieve and destroy any copies of the book." *United States v. Bolton*, 468 F. Supp. 3d 1, 4 (D.D.C. 2020). Notably, it did not name the publisher as a defendant. But while the court concluded that the book likely contained classified information, it refused to grant the government's request, remarking that "given the widespread dissemination of the books, the 'horse is already out of the barn.'" *Id.* at 6.

The government also sought an equitable remedy of constructive trust to seize any profits from the book, citing *Snepp*, as well as the terms of both security agreements. Bolton insisted that he had no reason to suspect that the book contained either SCI or any other kind of classified information. The court ruled that as to SF 312, but not SF 4414, his state of mind was irrelevant. *United States v. Bolton*, 496 F. Supp. 3d 146, 156 (D.D.C. 2020).

The court subsequently found, based on *ex parte* submissions from the government, that the book did in fact contain classified information, including SCI. But unlike the *Snowden* court, before ordering a forfeiture of profits, the court approved discovery by Bolton to try to show that the government acted in bad faith by delaying completion of its prepublication review and trying to influence classification decisions in order to avoid embarrassment for President Trump. *United States v. Bolton*, No. 20-cv-1580, 2021 WL 131445, at *5-8 (D.D.C. Jan. 14, 2021).

In its initial order refusing to stop publication, the court also suggested that Bolton might have broken the law, presumably including the Espionage Act (see casebook pp. 1234-1251). 468 F. Supp. 3d at 5. Not long afterward, a grand jury was convened to look into possible criminal violations. Katie Benner, *Justice Dept. Opens Criminal Inquiry into John Bolton's Book*, N.Y. Times, Sept. 16, 2020.

After Merrick Garland took over as Attorney General, the Justice Department closed its criminal investigation into Bolton and dropped its suit to recoup any profits from the book. Michael S. Schmidt & Katie Benner, *Justice Dept. Ends Criminal Inquiry and Lawsuit on John Bolton's Book*, N.Y. Times, June 16, 2021. In a statement about the settlement reached between Bolton and the DOJ — which included a pledge by DOJ never to sue Bolton over the book again — Bolton's attorney stated that by dropping the suit, "the Department of Justice has tacitly acknowledged that President Trump and his White House officials acted illegitimately." *Id.* Can you think of any other reasons the Garland Justice Department would decline to pursue either criminal or civil penalties against Bolton? Is such a prosecution a justifiable use of scarce prosecutorial resources? What kinds of information would civil discovery or criminal prosecution open to public scrutiny? Are there any reasons the Biden administration's Justice Department would be reluctant to make that information public?

[NSL p. 1271. Insert at the end of Note 9.]

In one of its rare pronouncements about FOIA, in 2021 the Supreme Court denied access to "draft" biological opinions from the Fish and Wildlife Service and National Marine Fisheries Service concerning the effect of a proposed EPA rule on certain endangered species. Such interagency communications were predecisional and deliberative, said the Court, and therefore protected by Exemption 5, because they were not officially regarded as final by either service that wrote them, even though they reflected the last views of each agency, and because the proposed EPA rule they addressed subsequently changed. *U.S. Fish and Wildlife Serv. v. Sierra Club, Inc.*, 141 S. Ct. 777 (2021). How do you think this ruling might affect the ability of a FOIA requester to learn about interagency communications regarding, say, the national security implications of a wall along the U.S.-Mexico border or the environmental impacts of a proposed new weapons system?

[NSL p. 1285. Insert after Note 6.]

6.1. A Too Secret Spy Court? The Foreign Intelligence Surveillance Court (FISC) and the Foreign Intelligence Surveillance Court of Review (FISCR) are responsible for approving and overseeing investigations conducted under the Foreign Intelligence Surveillance Act, as analyzed extensively in casebook Chapters 21 and 22. Because these courts are concerned entirely with issues affecting national security, their decisions are rarely published. Only in recent years has either court made some of its opinions public (albeit sometimes partially or heavily redacted) in matters relating to its jurisdiction, the constitutionality of certain intelligence procedures, and intelligence agencies' compliance with those procedures.

The 2015 USA Freedom Act requires the DNI to "conduct a declassification review of each decision, order, or opinion issued by [either court] that includes a significant construction or interpretation of any provision of law, . . . and, consistent with that review, make [it] publicly available to the greatest extent practicable." Pub. L. No. 114-23, §402(a)(2), 129 Stat. 268, 281 (codified at 50 U.S.C. §1872(a)). The DNI may, in the alternative, issue an unclassified summary of the legal analysis in an opinion. *Id.*, 129 Stat. at 281-282 (codified at 50 U.S.C. §1872(c)).

Many of the courts' opinions issued before the USA Freedom Act took effect remain entirely secret, however. In 2013, the ACLU and two law school groups filed suit in the FISC asserting that the First Amendment requires public access to certain FISC opinions addressing bulk collection of data, except where redactions are needed to serve a compelling government interest, like national security. Seven years later (after significant procedural maneuvering), a FISC judge rejected the plaintiffs' First Amendment claim on the merits, but the FISCR dismissed on the ground that *both* courts lack jurisdiction to even entertain such a claim. *In re Opinions & Orders by the FISC Addressing Bulk Collection of Data under the Foreign Intelligence Surveillance Act*, 957 F.3d 1344 (FISA Ct. of Rev. 2020) (per curiam).

In 2016, the same plaintiffs again sued in the FISC for release of opinions containing significant legal analysis, once again asserting a First Amendment right of access. This time both the FISC and FISCR concluded that they lacked jurisdiction. *In re Opinions and Orders of This Court Containing Novel or Significant Interpretations of Law*, No. Misc. 16-01, 2020 WL 5637419 (FISA Ct. Sept. 15, 2020), *aff'd.*, No. Misc. 20-02, 2020 WL 6888073 (FISA Ct. Rev. Nov. 19, 2020).

The ACLU then asked the Supreme Court to consider its First Amendment claim, which it based on both "history" and "logic": other federal courts have routinely published opinions about the scope and lawfulness of FISA surveillance without jeopardizing national security, many FISC opinions have been published, and publication of others would "play a significant positive role and would not compromise the operation of the FISC or the government's legitimate interest in protecting the confidentiality of properly classified information." Petition for Writ of Certiorari at 8, *ACLU v. United States*, No. 20-1499 (U.S. filed Apr. 19, 2021).

According to attorneys for the ACLU, "The unwarranted secrecy surrounding the surveillance court means that surveillance power can grow invisibly and easily become unmoored from the democratic consent that gives it legitimacy." David D. Cole, Jameel Jaffer & Theodore B. Olsen, Opinion, *A Spy Court Too Cloaked in Secrecy*, N.Y. Times, June 3, 2021. Do you agree that unlimited discretion in the executive branch to keep FISC opinions entirely secret poses such a threat? If the FISC has jurisdiction to rule on a First Amendment access claim, can you describe criteria for it to adjudicate such a claim? Do you think, for example, that the First Amendment compels disclosure at least of those portions of FISC rulings that include significant legal opinions?

[NSL p. 1293. Add at the end of the first paragraph of Note 5c.]

Legislation introduced, but not acted on, in 2020 would have expanded this procedure to cover the House. Protecting Our Democracy Act, H.R. 8363, S. 4880, 116th Cong. §403(a) (2020).

[NSL p. 1295. Insert at the end of footnote 1.]

The Supreme Court concluded that neither Article II nor the Supremacy Clause categorically precludes the issuance of a state criminal subpoena to a sitting President, citing Chief Justice John Marshall's ruling riding circuit in the treason trial of Aaron Burr, *United States v. Burr*, 25 F. Cas. 30 (C.C.D. Va. 1807) (No. 14692D), and the Nixon tapes case, *United States v. Nixon*, 418 U.S. 683 (1974). *Trump v. Vance*, 140 S. Ct. 2412, 2421-2425 (2020). The Court also decided that compliance by the President would not necessarily impair his ability to perform his constitutional functions by distracting him from his duties, tarnishing his reputation, or making him a target of harassment. *Id.* at 2425-2429. On remand, the district court found that the subpoena was reasonable and not issued in bad faith, 480 F. Supp. 3d 460 (S.D.N.Y. 2020), and the Second Circuit affirmed. 977 F.3d 198 (2d Cir. 2020). Finally, a year and a half after the grand jury subpoena was issued, the Supreme Court finally refused to stay its enforcement, *Trump v. Vance*, 141 S. Ct. 1364 (2021) (mem.), and the Manhattan District Attorney received the former President's financial records. *See* Jonah E. Bromwich, *Manhattan D.A. Now Has Trump's Tax Returns*, N.Y. Times, Feb. 25, 2021; Quinta Jurecic & Bryce Klehm, *Whither the Trump Financial Documents Cases?*, Lawfare, Mar. 2, 2021.

[NSL p. 1295. Insert at the end of the second full paragraph.]

A parallel suit by the President, seeking to quash similar subpoenas from the House Committees on Intelligence and Financial Services that sought information from Capital One and Deutsche Bank, was also stayed and combined with the earlier one. *Id.* The Supreme Court, noting the unprecedented nature of the case, then ruled that the House committees were not required to demonstrate a specific need for the records they sought, nor to show that the records were demonstrably critical to a legislative purpose. *Trump v. Mazars USA, LLP*, 140 S. Ct. 2019, 2032-2033 (2020). The information sought was private, the Court observed, which by definition did not implicate sensitive executive branch deliberations that might justify the invocation of executive privilege. *Id.* at 2033. Nevertheless, it concluded, "[w]ithout limits on its subpoena powers, Congress could 'exert an imperious controul' over the Executive Branch and aggrandize itself at the President's expense, just as the Framers feared," quoting *The Federalist No. 71*, at 484 (A. Hamilton). 140 S. Ct. at 2034. So saying, the Court found that in this case "the subpoenas do not represent a run-of-the-mill legislative effort but rather a clash between rival branches of government over records of intense political interest for all involved." *Id.*

The Court concluded that courts must take "adequate account of the separation of powers principles at stake, including both the significant legislative interests of Congress and the 'unique position' of the President." *Id.* at 2035 (citation omitted). They must, for example, avoid "constitutional confrontation between the two branches . . . whenever possible." *Id.* To that end, a subpoena should be "no broader than reasonably necessary to support Congress's legislative objective" and must "advance[ ] a valid legislative purpose." *Id.* at 2036. The House committees had described their objectives as "efforts to close loopholes that allow corruption, terrorism, and money laundering to infiltrate our country's financial system," as well as reforms to counter "foreign efforts to undermine the U.S. political process." *Id.* at 2027. In addition, the Court declared, a court must carefully scrutinize the burden on the President imposed by "a rival political branch that has an ongoing relationship with the President and incentives to use subpoenas for institutional advantage." *Id.* The Court then remanded for reconsideration by the lower courts, applying these standards.

No further action was taken in these cases before the subpoenas expired with the end of the 116th Congress in January 2021. *See Trump v. Mazars USA, LLP*, 832 Fed. App'x 6 (D.C. Cir. 2020) (mem.); Jurecic & Klehm, *supra*. On February 25, 2021, Congress renewed the subpoenas. *See* Alison Durkee, *House Lawmakers Reissue Subpoena for Trump's Financial Records to His Accounting Firm*, Forbes, Mar. 2, 2021. How do you think a court will apply the criteria set forth in the

Supreme Court's ruling? Should it matter that Donald J. Trump is no longer President?

––––––––––––––

[NSL p. 1296. Insert at the end of the carryover paragraph.]

The D.C. Circuit en banc eventually ruled that the House committee had standing to sue but remanded the case to a three-judge panel, which dismissed without addressing the immunity issues. *Comm. on the Judiciary v. McGahn*, 973 F.3d 121 (D.C. Cir. 2020). The panel concluded in a 2-1 vote that the committee lacked a cause of action. "When a party seeks to assert an implied cause of action under the Constitution itself," the court declared, "separation-of-powers principles are or should be central to the analysis, and usually Congress should decide whether to authorize a lawsuit." *Id.* at 123 (quoting *Ziglar v. Abbasi*, 137 S. Ct. 1843, 1857 (2017) (internal quotation marks omitted)). The court then decided that Congress *impliedly denied* such suits when in 1978 it approved them for the Senate but not the House. 973 F.3d at 123. The court concluded, "[T]his decision does not preclude Congress (or one of its chambers) from ever enforcing a subpoena in federal court; it simply precludes it from doing so without first enacting a statute authorizing such a suit." *Id.* at 125-126. Can the panel's conclusion be squared with the Supreme Court's ruling in *McGrain*, 273 U.S. at 174, that "[t]he power of inquiry — with process to enforce it — is an essential and appropriate auxiliary to the legislative function"?

The House committee appealed the panel's ruling to the en banc court, also disputing McGahn's claim of absolute testimonial immunity. The court agreed to rehear the case en banc and vacated the panel opinion. But the committee subsequently agreed that it would not pursue its case after McGahn said he would appear and provide limited testimony. *See* Charlie Savage, *McGahn to Testify on Trump and Investigation*, N.Y. Times, May 25, 2021. On July 13, 2021, the en banc D.C. Circuit agreed to dismiss the appeal (leaving the panel opinion vacated). *Comm. on the Judiciary v. McGahn*, No. 19-5331, Order at 1 (D.C. Cir. July 13, 2021) (en banc).

In one additional case with national security implications that arose during the Trump administration, the House Judiciary Committee sought information redacted from the Justice Department's 2019 Mueller Report about efforts to obstruct investigation into Russian interference in the 2016 presidential election. After lower courts approved access to that information, *In re Comm. on the Judiciary, U.S. House of Representatives*, 951 F.3d 589 (D.C. Cir. 2020), the Supreme Court stayed their orders and granted certiorari, *Dep't of Justice v. House Comm. on the Judiciary*, 141 S. Ct. 185 (2020) (mem.). But in November 2020, the House committee asked the Court to delay its consideration of the case until after the then-pending inauguration of President Biden. Melissa Quinn, *Supreme Court Delays Hearing Fight over Mueller Investigation Grand Jury Materials*, CBS News, Nov. 20, 2020. The Court agreed, and eventually agreed to vacate the decision below and remand with instructions to dismiss on mootness grounds. *See Dep't of Justice v. House Comm. on the Judiciary*, No. 19-1328, 2021 WL 2742772 (U.S. July 2, 2021).

Why do you suppose the committee wanted to postpone, or perhaps avoid, a ruling by the Supreme Court?

[NSL p. 1302. Insert after the third full paragraph.]

A dramatic retelling of the *New York Times*'s review of the *Pentagon Papers* and its decision to publish, with first-hand accounts from many of the reporters, editors, and lawyers involved, may be found in *The Pentagon Papers at 50: A Special Report*, N.Y. Times, June 9, 2021 (special section).

[NSL p. 1323. Insert after Note 4.]

5. Going Directly to the Source? In several cases described above, the government used criminal investigations to elicit information about sources of apparent leaks. But it also has secretly collected information directly from either reporters or from suspected sources.

In mid-2021, numerous media outlets began publishing stories documenting aggressive investigations by the Trump Justice Department in 2020 into sources of classified information leaks in early 2017. The government secretly secured court orders to collect phone and email metadata (discussed in Chapters 23 and 24) for reporters at the *New York Times*, *Washington Post*, and CNN as a means of identifying the reporters' confidential sources. It was successful in securing the phone records it sought, but not email data from *Times* and *Post* reporters. CNN ultimately agreed to turn over "a limited set of email logs" after months of litigation. *See* Devlin Barrett, *Trump Justice Department Secretly Obtained Post Reporters' Phone Records*, Wash. Post, May 7, 2021; Charlie Savage & Katie Benner, *Trump Administration Secretly Seized Phone Records of Times Reporters*, N.Y. Times, June 2, 2021. Katelyn Polantz & Evan Perez, *Trump Administration Pursued CNN Reporter's*

Records in Months-Long Secret Court Battle, CNN, June 9, 2021. An accounting of all that was publicly known about these investigations at this writing, as well as what remained undisclosed, is set forth in Bruce D. Brown & Gabe Rottman, *Everything We Know About the Trump-Era Records Demands from the Press*, Lawfare, July 6, 2021.

Government investigators also secretly collected account information in 2018 from Apple belonging to at least two Democratic members of Congress — Rep. Adam Schiff and Rep. Eric Swalwell, prominent critics of President Trump — as well as their staffs and family members. *See* Krishnadev Calamur & Ryan Lucas, *The Justice Department Watchdog Will Review a Trump-Era Probe of Democratic Lawmakers*, NPR, June 11, 2021. Apple was served with a subpoena issued by a federal grand jury. The Justice Department's Inspector General has announced that he will review the seizure of the lawmakers' records. Matt Zapotosky, Felicia Sonmez & Karoun Demirjian, *Justice Dept. Watchdog to Probe Trump-Era Leak Investigations, Including Secret Subpoenas for Data from Congress, Journalists*, Wash. Post, June 11, 2021.

The records requests to the *Times* and CNN were accompanied by nondisclosure (gag) orders, preventing the recipients from informing either the public or the individuals whose records were at issue. For a first-person account of CNN's months-long efforts to resist disclosure of Pentagon reporter Barbara Starr's communications records while under a gag order, see David Vigilante, *CNN Lawyer Describes Gag Order and Secretive Process Where Justice Department Sought Reporter's Email Records*, CNN, June 9, 2021.

For reasons explored in Chapter 39, such investigative moves are highly unusual and subject to special oversight procedures. Under Justice Department policy in place at the time, investigators must exhaust other investigative steps before seeking journalists' communication records, and the Attorney General must approve such investigative steps. At this writing, it is not known whether these policy requirements were met.

In the wake of these revelations, President Biden remarked that it is "simply, simply wrong" for the government to go after journalists' communications records. The White House and the Justice Department both later confirmed that the President's comment was not an off-the-cuff statement; it announced a policy shift. *See* Charlie Savage, *White House Seems to Affirm Biden's Vow to Bar Seizures of Reporters' Phone Data*, N.Y. Times, May 24, 2021; Veronica Stracqualursi, *Biden's Justice Department Says It Will No Longer Seize Reporters' Records for Leak Investigations*, CNN, June 5, 2021. The announcement represents a significant departure from the recent trend of relatively aggressive pursuit of leakers that began under the George W. Bush administration, continued through the Obama administration, and apparently reached new heights with the Trump administration's records requests.

Justice Department regulations provide that "[i]n determining whether to seek information from, or records of, members of the news media, the approach in every instance must be to strike the proper balance among several vital interests . . . [including] safeguarding the essential role of the free press in fostering government accountability and an open society." 28 C.F.R. §50.10(a)(2) (2021). How do you think DOJ investigators should weigh the cost of such collection — chilling both leakers and reporters alike — against the benefits? When would it be better to let leakers go unpunished rather than to violate reporter-source confidentiality? Should government officials ever decline to investigate leaks to the media of damaging national security information? How might the DOJ guidelines be enforced?

Some commentators have observed that the targets of these data requests are mostly individuals former President Trump considered political enemies. *See, e.g.,* Barbara McQuade, Opinion, *Did DOJ Target Trump Enemies Using Improper Subpoenas? We Need to Find Out,* MSNBC, June 11, 2021. If the investigations can be shown to have been politically motivated, what is the remedy? What laws or policies could be implemented to prevent such politicization in the future?

[CTL p. 5. Insert after the second paragraph.]

In 2021, the National Intelligence Council described the future of terrorism in this way:

> During the next 20 years, regional and intrastate conflicts, demographic pressures, environmental degradation, and democratic retrenchment are likely to exacerbate the political, economic, and social grievances terrorists have long exploited to gain supporters as well as safe havens to organize, train, and plot. These accelerants, the intensity and effects of which are likely to be uneven across different regions and countries, probably will also foster rural to urban international migration, further straining state resources and diminishing global and local counterterrorism efforts. [Nat'l Intelligence Council, *Global Trends 2040* (Mar. 2021), at 107.]

[CTL p. 6. Insert after comparison chart.]

See also Robert O'Harrow Jr., Andrew Ba Tran & Derek Hawkins, *The Rise in Domestic Extremism in America*, Wash. Post, Apr. 12, 2021 (reporting that since 2015, right-wing extremists have been involved in 267 plots or attacks causing 91 fatalities, while left-wing extremists accounted for 66 incidents causing 19 fatalities).

[CTL p. 7. Insert after carryover paragraph.]

After the January 6, 2021 riot at the Capitol, the intelligence community in March 2021 "assesse[d] that domestic violent extremists (DVEs) who are motivated by a range of ideologies and galvanized by recent political and societal events in the United States pose an elevated threat to the Homeland in 2021." *See* Off. of the Dir. of Nat'l Intelligence, *Domestic Violent Extremism Poses Heightened Threat in 2021* (Mar. 1, 2021), *quoted in National Strategy for Countering Domestic Terrorism* 10-11 (June 2021) (this Supplement at p. XX). But it also continued to predict that "that lone offenders or small cells of DVEs adhering to a diverse set of violent extremist ideologies are more likely to carry out violent attacks in the Homeland than organizations that allegedly advocate a DVE ideology." *Id.*

[CTL p. 97. Insert at the bottom of the page.]

In December 2018, President Trump announced the full withdrawal of some 2,000-2,500 U.S. military forces still in Syria, prompting the resignation of Defense Secretary James Mattis. *See* Mark Landler, Helene Cooper & Eric Schmitt, *Trump Withdraws U.S. Forces From Syria, Declaring "We Have Won Against ISIS"*, N.Y. Times, Dec. 19, 2018; Helene Cooper, *Jim Mattis, Defense Secretary, Resigns in Rebuke of Trump's Worldview*, N.Y. Times, Dec. 20, 2018. Two months later, the White House declared that about 200 troops would remain as a "peacekeeping force." Alex Johnson, *U.S. to Leave about 200 Troops in Syria, White House Says*, NBC News, Feb. 21, 2019. Nevertheless, an estimated 800 remained there a year later. Miriam Berger, *Where U.S. Troops Are in the Middle East and Afghanistan, Visualized*, Wash. Post, Jan. 4, 2020. In September 2020, the Pentagon sent another 100 troops, armored vehicles, and other equipment to Syria to counter Russian activities, on the same day that Trump declared that U.S. forces "are out of Syria" except for those guarding oil fields in the region. Eric Schmitt, *U.S. Sending More Troops to Syria to Counter the Russians*, N.Y. Times, Sept. 18, 2020.

In November 2020, the State Department's Special Representative for Syria Engagement, James F. Jeffrey, revealed that the number of U.S. troops remaining in Syria was "a lot more than" the 200 authorized by President Trump. "We were always playing shell games to not make clear to our leadership how many troops we had there," he said. Katie Bo Williams, *Outgoing Syria Envoy Admits Hiding US Troop Numbers*, Defense One, Nov. 12, 2020. Presumably, however, the Defense Department always knew how many of its personnel were deployed in the country. In May 2021, nearly 1,000 U.S. troops reportedly remained in eastern Syria to fight remnants of ISIS forces and prevent them from regrouping. Lolita C. Baldor, *US Central Command Chief: Important to Keep Pressure on ISIS*, AP, May 23, 2021.

What does this record suggest about the Commander in Chief's ability to execute U.S. foreign policy or to direct the use of its armed forces? About the ability of Congress and the American public to monitor U.S. military activities abroad and to hold government officials accountable for those activities?

In February 2021, President Biden ordered air strikes against targets in Syria in response to rocket attacks by Iranian-backed militias on U.S. forces in Iraq. In a report to Congress under the War Powers Resolution, he said he acted "consistent with my responsibility to protect United States citizens both at home and abroad and in furtherance of United States national security and foreign policy interests, pursuant to my constitutional authority to conduct United States foreign relations and as Commander in Chief and Chief Executive." But he did not invoke either the 2001 AUMF or the 2002 Iraq War resolution. The White House, Letter to the Speaker of the House and President Pro Tempore of the Senate Consistent with the War Powers Resolution (Feb. 27, 2021). The report also claimed that "[t]he United States took this action pursuant to the United States' inherent right of self-defense as reflected in Article 51 of the United Nations Charter." And it declared U.S. readiness to use force when "the government of [a] state . . . is unwilling or unable to prevent the use of its territory by non-state militia groups" to attack "our personnel and our partners." Can you briefly cite authorities for each of these claims? *See* Rebecca Ingber, *Legally Sliding into War*, Just Security, Mar. 15, 2021 (expressing doubt about such claims).

[CTL p. 100. Insert before Summary of Basic Principles.]

In July 2020, members of both parties introduced a far more modest proposal:

H.R. 7500
116th Cong., 2d Sess.
July 9, 2020

Sec. 1. Short title.

This Act may be cited as the "Limit on the Expansion of the Authorization for Use of Military Force Act".

Sec. 2. Limitation on expansion of the 2001 authorization for use of military force.

The Authorization for Use of Military Force (Public Law 107-40; 50 U.S.C. 1541 note) may not be construed to provide authorization for the use of force, including under section 5(b) of the War Powers Resolution (50 U.S.C. 1544(b)), in any country in which United States Armed Forces are not engaged in hostilities pursuant to such Authorization as of the date of the enactment of this Act.

Sec. 3. Rule of construction.

Nothing in this Act may be construed —

(1) to deem the use of force in any country in which United States Armed Forces are engaged in hostilities as of the date of the enactment of this Act as lawful or unlawful pursuant to the Authorization for Use of Military Force (Public Law 107-40; 50 U.S.C. 1541 note); or
(2) as an authorization for use of military force.

According to the sponsors of H.R. 7500, "In the event that the president must act to defend the United States in a country where we are not operating today, he could do so under the terms laid out in the War Powers Resolution of 1973." Anthony Brown et al., Opinion, *Bipartisan Lawmakers Introduce Bill to Limit Further Expansion of 2001 Authorization for Use of Military Force*, The Hill, July 9, 2020. Can you describe the circumstances under which this statement might be true?

Did this measure answer the objections raised by President Trump a year earlier? Can you guess why the bill never made it out of committee?

[CTL p. 912. Insert at end of Note 4.]

In *Kaplan v. Lebanese Canadian Bank, SAL*, 999 F.3d 842 (2d Cir. 2021), the Second Circuit revisited *Halberstam*, refining and arguably relaxing the elements of JASTA aiding-and-abetting liability. According to the appeals court, JASTA does *not* require "awareness," as the lower court held in *Kaplan*. "While the word 'aware' normally denotes full recognition of the existence or qualities of an object or circumstance, *Halberstam*'s attachment of the 'generally' modifier imparts to the concept 'generally aware' a connotation of something less than full, or fully focused, recognition." *Id.* at 863. The court found it sufficient that multiple public sources available to the defendant bank identified its customers as integral parts of a foreign terrorist organization that was carrying out rocket attacks on civilians. *See also Gonzalez v. Google LLC*, No. 18-16700, 2021 WL 2546675, at *23 (9th Cir. June 22, 2021) ("[A]llegations indicating Google knowingly contributed money to [by sharing advertising revenues with] ISIS [the designated foreign terrorist organization Islamic State in Iraq and Syria] suffice to show that Google understood it played a role in the violent and life-endangering activities undertaken by ISIS, and therefore establish the second element of aiding-and-abetting liability for purposes of §2333(d)(2)."). JASTA aiding-and-abetting liability does require "actual knowledge," the court added.

> But the actual knowledge component of the *Halberstam* standard requires that the defendant "know[]" that it is providing "assistance," 18 U.S.C. §2333(d)(2) — whether directly to the FTO or indirectly through an intermediary . . . . That knowledge component "is designed to avoid" imposing liability on "innocent, incidental participants." *Halberstam*, 705 F.2d at 485 n.14. If the defendant knowingly — and not innocently or inadvertently — gave assistance, directly or indirectly, and if that assistance was substantial, then aiding and abetting is sufficiently established if the defendant was "*generally* aware" that it was playing a role in international terrorism. [*Kaplan*, 999 F.3d at 863-864.]

See Gonzales, 2021 WL 2546675, at *25 (allegations that "Google reviewed and approved ISIS videos for monetization and thereby knowingly provided ISIS with financial assistance for its terrorist operations . . . despite its awareness that these videos were created by

ISIS and posted by ISIS using known ISIS accounts . . . are sufficient to plausibly allege that Google's assistance was knowing as required by §2333(d)(2)").

The role of social media in, and potential JASTA liability for, facilitating acts of international terrorism was hotly debated by a divided panel in *Gonzales*, a debate complicated by the statutory immunity afforded some media by section 230 of the Communications Decency Act. 47 U.S.C. §230.

[CTL p. 913. Insert at the end of Note 5.]

See also Gonzalez v. Google LLC, No. 18-16700, 2021 WL 2546675, at *24 (9th Cir. June 22, 2021) ("Google's sharing of revenues with members of ISIS does not, by itself, support the inference that Google tacitly agreed to commit homicidal terrorist acts with ISIS, where [decedent's] murder was an overt act perpetrated pursuant to, and in furtherance of, that common scheme.").

[CTL p. 942. Insert before Summary of Basic Principles.]

4. Civil Liability for the Lafayette Park "Clearing." On June 1, 2020, law enforcement authorities forcibly cleared Lafayette Park (across from the White House) of persons protesting the murder of George Floyd. Clearing the protesters enabled President Donald Trump to cross the Park to visit a nearby church where he displayed a Bible for the media. Some of the protesters sued the President, Attorney General William Barr, and other federal and local law enforcement officers for their role in clearing the Park, asserting claims under §1985(3), among others.

On motions to dismiss the complaint, the district court held that the plaintiffs did not plausibly plead the element of agreement, necessary for their §1985(3) claim.

> The non-conclusory allegations on which the plaintiffs contend an agreement can be inferred include the following: before Lafayette Square was cleared, President Trump's Twitter posts "threatened to use and encouraged violence against protesters"; President Trump directed Barr to "personally lead the response to the unrest"; Barr requested "'riot teams' and other specialized agents" from other federal agencies; on June 1, law enforcement officers met at the Joint Operations Command Center at Lafayette Square; before the Square was cleared,

Barr was seen meeting with federal law enforcement personnel and "pointing north towards St. John's Church"; federal, D.C., and Arlington officers used the same type of force to disperse demonstrators; and Barr and [Secretary of Defense Mark] Esper walked with the President to St. John's Church after the Square was cleared.

These allegations, taken as true, do not show sufficient "events, conversations, or documents indicating an agreement or meeting of the minds' amongst the defendants to violate [plaintiffs'] rights based on [their] membership in a protected class." *Barber v. D.C. Gov't*, 394 F. Supp. 3d 49, 66 (D.D.C. 2019) (alteration and internal quotation marks omitted). Rather, they demonstrate only that these officials were communicating with each other on June 1, prior to and after the clearing of Lafayette Square. Merely alleging that the defendant officials communicated, without alleging any details of those communications that suggest an unlawful agreement, cannot justify inferring the requisite agreement for a §1985(3) conspiracy. [*Black Lives Matter DC v. Trump*, No. 20-cv-1469, 2021 WL 2530722, at *12 (D.D.C. June 21, 2021).]

However, the court refused to dismiss the plaintiffs' claims under the Civil Rights Act, 42 U.S.C. §1983, against local police officers who assisted in clearing the protesters. Section 1983 provides a civil action against state and local officials (but not against federal officials) who violate a plaintiff's constitutional or other federal rights. The court reasoned that allegations "that the plaintiffs were engaged in a peaceful protest when federal and Arlington defendants 'destroy[ed] the peaceable gathering' with unprovoked force" plausibly alleged an unconstitutional restriction on protected speech, as well as unlawful retaliation for exercise of First Amendment rights. *Id.* at *16-17, 19. It found that these rights were sufficiently "clearly established" at the time of the protests to overcome defendants' qualified immunity defense at the pleading stage.

5. Civil Liability for the January 6, 2021, Capitol Riot. U.S. Capitol Police officers who were injured in the January 6, 2021, riot have sued former President Trump and others for their alleged role in instigating the riots. *See* Mike Ives, *Two Capitol Police Officers Sue Trump Over January Riot*, N.Y. Times, Mar. 31,2021, updated Apr. 6, 2021. The complaint is available at https://int.nyt.com/data/documenttools/blassingame-hemby-20210330-complaint-redacted/cf9b4d8c6cd401c6/full.pdf.

A complaint invoking the Ku Klux Klan Act has also been filed by a member of Congress against the former President, Rudolph W. Giuliani, the "Proud Boys," "Oathkeepers," and others who participated in the riot. That complaint is available at https://www.washingtonpost.com/

context/thompson-v-trump-et-al/ee4a2b71-cdf1-4f64-9778-422dbd480172/.
